Behold The Bridegroom Cometh

By
James F. Webb

© Copyright 2004, James F. Webb

All Rights Reserved.

No part of this book may be reproduced, stored in a retrieval system, or transmitted by any means, electronic, mechanical, photocopying, recording, or otherwise, without written permission from the author.

ISBN: 1-59453-427-6

Index

Chapter	Title	Page
1	The Surety of His Coming	1
2	Calendars and Such	9
3	The Promise of the Coming Messiah	17
4	The Birth and Early Years of Jesus	25
5	The Earthly Ministry of Christ	31
6	The Day of the Cross	45
7	Are there Signs of His Return?	61
8	More Specific Examples of the Signs of the Times	71
9	The Sign of the Times of the Gentiles, and the Seventy Years	79
10	The Rapture of the Church	105
11	The Judgment Seat of Christ and the Marriage of the Lamb	113
12	The Coming of Antichrist and Tribulation	121
13	The Great Tribulation and the Appearance of Christ	143
14	The Golden Millennium and Beyond	157
15	The Great White Throne Judgment	169
16	The Eternal City and the New World	179
17	Are You Ready?	197

Chart	Title	Page
1	The Basic Jewish Calendar	11
2	Alignment of the Sacred and Civil Year Months in the Jewish Calendar	14
3	Alignment of the Great Two Weeks and the Eight Days of Man	15
4	The Day of the Cross	49
5	The Week of the Cross	55
6	Jewish National Freedom	81

7	The Intervals of 69 (approximate values)	82
8	Jerusalem and the Times of the Gentiles	85
9	The 2,553-Year Intervals and the 70-Year Intervals	93
10	Comparison of the Thirty-Nine Years of Joseph with the Days of Noah	100
11	The Three Trinities (God, Man, & Satan)	135
12	Division of the New World	183
13	The Corners of the Pyramid	188
14	The New World	191
15	The Street, the River, and the Tree of Life	195

Chapter 1
The Surety of His Coming

On a warm, pleasant day, approximately the eighteenth of May according to our calendar, an uncertain number of people left Jerusalem through an eastern gate and moved down into the Kidron Valley, followed the road as it emerged from the lower terrain, and began to circle the southern bank of the mountain called Olivet in the direction of the small village of Bethany. Behind them, the panorama of the walled city spread out, dominated by the massive stones of the temple of Herod, and the Antonia fortress which adjoined the temple grounds along a portion of the northwest wall.

There were other travelers along the way that day for the weather was pleasant and the sky was clear—with the exception of some white fluffy clouds which offered welcome shade now and then. But as the particular group walked, several spoke among themselves in low voices, their words demonstrating a degree of sadness as though their preference would have desired that this certain day may have been postponed for another time yet in the future.

Before the village of Bethany actually came into view, the leader of the group led them away from the well-traveled road and directed their steps upward through the many rows of olive trees, from which the mountain received its name. There, the leader stepped a small distance away from the others and turned to face them.

He spoke to them in simple but urgent sentences as though he were going away for a while and wanted to make sure they fully understood what they were to accomplish during his absence. But Luke's written account in Acts seems to infer that, even at this time, at least some of the people present in that company may not have completely comprehended the reason for the walk to the top of the Mount of Olives, or the fact that he was actually going away for what was, in the eyes of men, a lengthy span of time.

Almost like children who yearned in their hearts for a thing very dear to them, they asked Jesus, *"Lord, will thou at this time restore again the kingdom to Israel?"*

His answer was a reminder of a conversation he had held with his disciples about forty-four hours before as they had sat upon this very mountain.

"It is not for you to know the times or the seasons, which the Father hath put in his own power," he said, then continued, *"But ye shall receive power, after that the Holy Ghost is come upon you: and ye shall be witnesses unto me both in Jerusalem, and in all Judea, and in Samaria, and unto the uttermost part of the world."*

He raised his hands to bless them, and, as he did so, to the utter amazement of those who were before him, his feet actually lifted above the surface of earth and he rose into the very air over them, entirely freed from the bounds of gravity this world laid upon all others men. Upward he rose as an eagle rising above the land, Bethany coming into view a short distance away and Jerusalem visible to the east. Even in those moments, he must have sensed the hatred still festering in the hearts of the temple hierarchy who had sought to end his influence over the masses by crucifying him on Golgotha. Even then, he was aware of the pain those people, and others like them, would inflict upon those who followed him, but he also looked forward through centuries of time and knew a better day would come in the future.

Eyes filled with the glory of the great miracle they were beholding, but moistened by the knowledge that he would no longer be with them physically, those whose feet were yet bound to the earth peered upward into the spring sky until he disappeared into one of the white clouds and was seen no more. Unwilling to let go of him, they continued to gaze upward, hoping for one more glimpse of the one they called Lord.

"And while they looked steadfastly toward heaven as he went up, behold, two men stood by them in white apparel; Which also said, Ye men of Galilee, why stand ye gazing up into heaven? this same Jesus, which is taken up from you into heaven, shall so come in like manner as ye have seen him go into heaven" **(Acts 1:10-11).**

Jesus Christ is coming back to the earth again, and in a very physical, visible form. Of all the many wonderful facts taught in the Bible, this amazing truth is one of the clearest revelations. Therefore, it seems to remain one of the greatest mysteries just why so many in the world refuse to accept Bible teaching at its simple and literal value, attempting to supplant all manner of substitute interpretations. But, even in this golden age of great scientific advancement, his return still remains the very blessed hope of the Church.

"Looking for that blessed hope, and the glorious appearing of the great God and our Savior Jesus Christ" **(Titus 2:13).**

But even among those who profess to believe in a visible and physical return of the Lord to the earth, there seems to be a differing opinion concerning just what is really meant. These differences fall into three major categories.

1. A-Millennialists
2. Post-Millennialists
3. Pre-Millennialists

All three categories deal with a certain time span known as the Millennium, a period of 1,000 years (designated in **Revelation, Chapter 20).** But the A-Millennialists take a negative approach. Although there are many varieties of this theological view, the basic element may be summed up in one concise statement—they do not believe in the Millennium at all. the belief is that history will continue "as it always has" in an unbroken chain of events as time marches on forever. All things will continue as they have from the beginning of creation, and the individual will eventually go to be with the Lord, the transition being accomplished at the event of death. At some unknown point in the extreme future, as science predicts, the immediate solar system may cease to exist when one of several cataclysmic events erases things as they now are. It is my own opinion that the theory of "reincarnation" would also be found among the A-Millennialists.

Post-Millennialists do believe in an actual return to the earth by the Lord, but only after mankind has successfully improved and elevated its spiritual and physical nature to a point where God will consider man good enough to dwell in his presence. This will come after man has flourished through 1,000 years of glorious peace and prosperity, brought about by man's advances in civilization and self-understanding.

This represents a supreme faith in the natural character of man. Starting from a lowly beginning, the natural "goodness" of man has enabled the human being to continuously better himself. Barring periodic setbacks, the overall station of the human race has steadily moved upward to more exemplary heights, proving the all-encompassing brotherhood of man, and that the race is a basically good, honest, moral, and honorable creation. The belief apparently ignores God's own prophetic picture of the history of man's civilization as depicted by the great image witnessed in a dream by Nebuchadnezzar in the second chapter of **Daniel**. It also seems to ignore many other familiar Bible verses: **Isaiah 64:6; Romans 3:23; Romans 7-18; Romans 8:8; 1Corinthians 2:14; John 8:44; Galatians 3:22; Galatians 5:17; 1John 3:8; 1John 3:8;** and others.

The Pre-Millennial view teaches that Christ will return to the earth in a physical, visible form before the Golden Millennium actually begins. This is the theory supported and advocated by this book. The simple truth is that it is the presence of the Lord in the world and ruling over it that makes it possible for the millennium of peace and prosperity to come into existence.

The references in the Bible to a Pre-Millennial return of Christ are plain and numerous, and should not be seriously ignored by anyone genuinely seeking the truth. For example, consider the account given in chapters nineteen and twenty of the book of Revelation, which describe the return of Jesus to the world following the seven years of tribulation.

"Immediately after the tribulation of those days shall the sun be darkened, and the moon shall not give her light, and the stars shall fall from heaven; and the powers of heaven shall be shaken; And then shall appear the sign of the Son of man in heaven: and then shall all the tribes of the earth mourn, and they shall see the Son of man coming in the clouds of heaven with power and great glory." **(Matthew 24:29-30).**

"And I saw heaven opened, and behold a white horse; and he that sat upon him was called Faithful and True, and in righteousness he

doth judge and make war. His eyes were as a flame of fire, and on his head were many crowns; and he had a name written, that no man knew, but he himself. And he was clothed with a vesture dipped in blood: and his name is called The word of God. And the armies which were in heaven followed him upon white horses, clothed in fine linen, white and clean. And out of his mouth goeth a sharp sword, that with it he should smite the nations: and he shall rule with a rod of iron: and he treadeth the winepress of the fierceness and wrath of Almighty God. And he hath on his vesture and on his thigh a name written, King of Kings, and Lord of Lords "**(Revelation 19:11-16).**

"And I saw the beast, and the kings of the earth, and their armies, gathered together to make war against him that sat on the horse, and against his army. And the beast was taken, and with him the false prophet that wrought miracles before him, with which he deceived them that had received the mark of the beast [Revelation 13], *and them that worshipped his image. These both were cast alive into a lake of fire burning with brimstone. And the remnant were slain with the sword of him that sat upon the horse, which sword proceeded out of his mouth* [Revelation 1:16]*: and all the fowls were filled with their flesh"* **(Revelation 19:19-21).**

"And I saw an angel come down from heaven, having the key of the bottomless pit and a great chain in his hand. And he laid hold on the dragon, that old serpent, which is the Devil, and Satan, and bound him a thousand years, and cast him into the bottomless pit, and shut him up, and set a seal upon him, that he should deceive the nations no more, till the thousand years should be fulfilled: and after that he must be loosed a little season. And I saw thrones, and they sat upon them, and judgment was given unto them: and I saw the souls of them that were beheaded for the witness of Jesus, and for the word of God, and which had not worshipped the beast, neither his image, neither had received his mark upon their foreheads, or in their hands; and they lived and reigned with Christ a thousand years. But the rest of the dead lived not again until the thousand years were finished. This is the first resurrection. Blessed and holy is he that hath part in the first resurrection: on such the second death hath no power [Revelation 20:14, and Revelation 21:8], *but they shall be priests of God and of*

Christ, and shall reign with him a thousand years. And when the thousand years are expired, Satan shall be loosed out of his prison, and shall go out to deceive the nations which are in the four quarters of the earth, Gog and Magog, to gather them together to battle: the number of whom is as the sands of the sea. And they went up on the breadth of the earth, and compassed the camp of the saints about, and the beloved city: and fire came down from God out of heaven, and devoured them. And the devil that deceived them was cast into the lake of fire and brimstone, where the beast and the false prophet are, and shall be tormented day and night for ever and ever" **(Revelation 20:1-10).**

In these verses of Scripture, the actual thousand years of the Millennium are mentioned at lease six times, and all occurring after the description of the return of the Lord in glory to the earth. In verse four of chapter twenty, it is stated that Christ will actually reign for the thousand year period. Many direct references are contained within the pages of the Bible relating to the Millennium, or Kingdom Age, but all necessitating the visible and physical return of the Savior to establish these things. The best dreams of man, the most notable ideas and intentions of the prowess of his hands, are doomed to inevitable failure if God is not in them. Man seeks a one-world government, expects it to be perfect, but would place an imperfect man at the head of it; man seeks to physically unite all religions of the world, but does not realize there is no successful union in mortal flesh. It is the reborn spiritual souls of the redeemed that truly enable the Church to be united, and that only in the Spirit of God.

The Golden Millennium is often compared to a Sabbath day in the traditional Jewish week. The Sabbath was the seventh day, or, in the American week, the day known as Saturday. To the Jew, it was observed as a day of rest by the direct order of God. The Millennial Kingdom will also be comparable to a day of rest to the mixed population that dwells on the earth during those years, for the world will experience the blessings of peace, prosperity, cures for those that are sick, freedom from the corruption and abusiveness of crime, and a perfect government in the person of Jesus Christ.

The theory that the Golden Millennium is a Sabbath day comes from the belief that the entire history of mankind upon the earth, counting from Adam and Eve, may be counted in seven great days of one-thousand years each. It is called the Great Week theory. It is usually joined with the seven days of the Creative Week to form the Great Two Weeks theory. Although most theologians accepting the theory of the one-thousand-year days are in concurrence with the Great Week following the expulsion of Adam and Eve from the Garden of Eden, they often disagree concerning the first seven days.

The first two chapters of the Book of Genesis discuss a period of time usually referred to as the Week of Creation. But many consider that the correct terminology for this period should be the Week of Restoration. The Pre-Adamic World, destroyed and made to be without form and void **(Genesis 1:2; Jeremiah 4:23-26)** by the rebellion of Lucifer against God, was restored by God to its original state. To do this, God used seven steps, denoted as days.

A world without light is a world without heat—a frozen and lifeless orb where even the very atmosphere lay on the surface in the form of ice. Then, as light was restored, the world began to thaw. The atmosphere reformed and the waters re-established the seas. Study the words and order of events given us in **Genesis**, and decide for yourself if they do not describe the rebirth of a planet from the clutches of a very frigid temperature.

Whether the reader chooses to believe the seven days given in **Genesis** depict the Creative Week, or, the Restorative Week, they are still counted as days. Therefore, those very same seven days, regardless of their exact length, are usually connected with the Great Week of Human History to form the Great Two Weeks. And, in theory, giving equal recognition to each of the "weeks," we find that the race of man (counting from Adam and Eve) will actually be on the earth for a total of a little over eight great days (Adam and Eve were created as the second act of God during the sixth day). This theory is called the "Eight Days of Man." See **Figure 3** in chapter two, where the theories are compared to the Jewish calendar.

I have especially mentioned the theories of the Great Weeks and the Eight Days of Man in this work because, if correct, they offer a very strong sign that the Second Coming of Christ is truly drawing very near.

The following pages contain material from several lessons I have taught through the years. In one way or the other, all relate to the Second Coming of the Lord. In the following chapters, I have attempted to impress the reader with numerous signs which seem to point to the nearness of the Rapture, the seven years of great tribulation to fall upon the earth, and the approach of the Lord's Kingdom here on this planet. In particular, I will direct the reader's attention to a special interval of years presented first in the Book of Genesis, then appearing in later history to tie events in the Old Testament to the Twentieth Century.

Since the different lessons were originally presented as separate works, the reader may find that some material may be repeated from time to time. I sincerely hope that those who read the things written in this book, will be blessed as much in studying them, as I was in writing them down. If, by some means, this work can instill in others a hunger to know more about God's Word, then I have been successful in my intention.

With love in Christ,

James F. Webb

Chapter 2
Calendars and Such

"And God said, Let there be lights in the firmament of the heavens to divide the day from the night; and let them be for signs, and for seasons, and for days, and years" **(Genesis 1:14).**

In all areas of the world, it has been found that most ancient civilizations made use of calendar systems, many of which showed a rather high degree of understanding concerning celestial mechanics. Chinese astronomers were very accurately predicting eclipses four-thousand years ago. The Babylonians were also quite skilled in astronomy, dividing their calendars into twelve months based upon the twelve signs of the zodiac.

On Salisbury Plain in southern England, the peculiar circles of monolithic stones known as Stonehenge was constructed as a device to measure the years, perhaps pointing to certain special feast or holy days. The Aztecs and Mayan civilizations developed very accurate methods to measure the years, the Mayan 18-month calendar actually presenting a calendar of 364.24 days.

The Egyptian civilization used a calendar consisting of twelve months, each month composed of thirty days. An additional five days were added at the close of the year to bring the total to 365. Some sources report that as early as twenty centuries before the birth of Christ a "leap year" was intercalated every four years to further correct their calendar. However, this custom seems to have been abandoned at some point during the following ages, for, in B.C. 238, the ruler of Egypt, Ptolemy III, attempted to reinstate the use of the leap year. He was firmly refused by the priests, who would not alter the cycle of the religious ceremonies.

Our own system of counting time officially originated with the Julian calendar. Julius Caesar, greatly aware of the discrepancies and confusion prevailing in the Roman calendar then in use, counseled with the Greek mathematician and astronomer Sosigines. The result was the revision of the existing calendar to 365.25 days. To achieve this value, the "leap year" was inserted every fourth year, just as we employ its use today. The Julian calendar went into effect on January 1, B.C. 45. Its use continued for over sixteen centuries, until time finally proved it to be slightly in error.

As centuries passed, the seasons drifted a little further off every year, until, in A.D. 1582, the season of Spring began as early as March 11. Pope Gregory XIII consulted with his astronomers, and the calendar was corrected by omitting the dates between October 4, 1582, and October 15, 1582.

The Gregorian calendar, which we use, today, is very similar to the Julian calendar in many ways. A standard year is 365 days long, and every fourth year is a leap year containing 366 days. However, the major difference is that in century years which are divisible by 400, the leap year is omitted. A further correction is to be made by dropping the leap year every 3,300 years.

The first reference to an actual calendar system in the Bible is found in the seventh and eighth chapters of Genesis. According to the eleventh verse of chapter seven, the Flood began upon the seventeenth day of the second month. When the waters were abated, the Ark came to rest upon the mountains of Ararat, according to **Genesis 8:4,** on the seventeenth day of the seventh month, exactly five months later. This period of time is given in **Genesis 7:24,** and **Genesis 8:3,** as 150 days, making the average month equal to thirty days. If the same number of days composed every month of the year, the length of the calendar year at that time would be 360 days.

The ancient Egyptians, we remember, employed a calendar of twelve months, each month containing thirty days, but added an additional five days at the year's end, therefore bringing the total value to 365 days. There is no way of knowing whether or not the calendar used at the time of the Flood was the same system used by the Egyptians.

According to Biblical chronology, the Flood occurred in B.C. 2348, whereas Moses wrote Genesis between B.C. 1491, and B.C. 1451, over 850 years later. The Biblical account does not make it absolutely clear whether Moses' references are to the calendar of

Noah's day, or simply a conversion over to the calendar of his own day.

The Jewish calendar, given by God to Moses, was based upon the movements of the moon. In order to approximate the uneven number of days in the orbit of the month, it utilized twelve months **(I Kings 4:7,** and **I Chronicles 27:1-15)** alternating between thirty and twenty-nine days, thus making the average month 29.5 days long. The names of the twelve Jewish months, with their corresponding number of days, are given in **Chart 1**. A special thirteenth month, is also shown in this figure.

CHART 1
THE BASIC JEWISH CALENDAR

SACRED YEAR ARRANGEMENT	CIVIL YEAR ARRANGEMENT	NAME OF MONTH	NO. OF DAYS	CORRESPONDING WITH:
1	7	Nisan (Abib)	30	April
2	8	Iyar	29	May
3	9	Sivan	30	June
4	10	Tammuz	29	July
5	11	Ab	30	August
6	12	Elul	29	September
7	1	Tishri (Ethanim)	30	October
8	2	Cheshvan (Bul, or Marcheshvan)	29	November
9	3	Kislev	30	December
10	4	Tebet	29	January
11	5	Shebat	30	February
12	6	Adar	29	March
13	—	Veadar (Adar Sheni)	29	March-April

The Basic Jewish Calendar employed 12 months of alternating 30 and 29-day lengths, with a special 13-month leap year intercalated 7 times in a 19-year cycle. The common 12-month year was 354-days long; the leap year was 383-days long. The average year, over the 19-year cycle, was 364.68421-days long. In usage, the Sacred Year began with the month Nisan, but a civil Year seems to have been used also (used today to calculate Jewish New Year) beginning with the month Tishri.

Six months of thirty days each plus six months of twenty-nine days each give a total value amounting to only 354 days. This is known as the common year. Modern application of this calendar varies the number of days in certain months, creating a defective, regular, or perfect (abundant) common year according as it has 353, 354, or 355 days. Since the tropical year, used in the Gregorian calendar, is 365,2422 days long, the basic Jewish calendar year of twelve months proves to be a little over eleven days short.

The calendar, if used in this fashion, would quickly throw the seasons off, causing the dates to fall about a week and a half earlier every year. Consequently, the basic Jewish calendar employed the special use of a "leap" year to adjust the system over a period of years. The leap year was composed of the twelve regular months of the common year plus the intercalation of a thirteenth month at special intervals. The leap-year month was called Adar Sheni (it was also known as Veadar, and also the Second Adar). It consisted of 29 days, therefore making the leap year 383 days long. In modern usage, the leap year is also described as being defective, regular, or perfect (abundant), according as it has 383, 384, or 385 days.

Regular years and leap years were spaced throughout a 19-year cycle, the calendar being arranged in such an order so that twelve years would be common years, and seven years would be leap years. The leap year was generally intercalated in the 3rd, 6th, 8th, 11th, 14th, 17th, and 19th years of the cycle. Used in this most rudimentary form, the total number of days contained in such a nineteen-year cycle is 6,929. This means the average year in this cycle would equal 364.68421 days. An exact tropical year in the Gregorian calendar amounts to 365.242196 days. Nineteen of these years equals 6,939.601724 total days, making the basic form of the Jewish calendar a little over ten days short. The modern Jewish calendar does not exhibit a discrepancy so great, for days are variously added or subtracted from certain months to make the system coincide quite well with the Gregorian.

"And the Lord spoke unto Moses and Aaron in the land of Egypt, saying, This month shall be unto you the beginning of months: it shall be the first month [April] of the year to you" **(Exodus 12:1-2).**

The sacred year began with the month Nisan, as dictated by God to Moses to mark the time of the Exodus. It is referred to throughout the Bible as the "first" month, and all other months are counted from this point. But modern usage, although yet referring to Nisan as the first month of the Holy year, places the official new year in the autumn, which is harvest time (certain Bible verses such as: **Exodus 23:16; 34:22;** and **Leviticus 25:4 & 9,** seem to imply that this custom may have been followed in earlier times). This "Civil" year, or rather year of agriculture, began upon the first day of the seventh month (usually October), which is the feast of Trumpets **(Numbers 29:1).**

As the first day of the holy year approached, certain Temple priests were appointed the task of observing the sky during the evening and night. Since their calendar was based on the phases of the moon, their job was to spot the first showing of the thin crescent new moon (the first new moon after the spring equinox). When that moment arrived, they were to notify the proper persons and the next day was declared the first day of the month of Nisan. I do not know if it was ever necessary, should a day or so still remain from the previous year, to simply delete the old year's days to make way for the new.

The Jewish calendar embodies several symbolic meanings within its structure. The leap year, employing the thirteenth month, or the Second Adar, seems to portray to us a making right of things. Christ is referred to as the Second Adam **(I Corinthians 15:45-47),** and Christ has made it possible for all things to be made right for mankind, if they will only accept his sacrifice.

Superstition has long designated the number thirteen as an unlucky number, probably originating from the fact that there were thirteen people in the upper room the evening that Judas Iscariot betrayed Christ. But, especially in the case of Jesus, and the upper room, the number thirteen, rather than being thought of as an unlucky number, is better thought of as a number illustrating the inadequacy of mortal man, and his utter dependency on the mercy of God. The Son of God, the promised Messiah, had appeared to men and offered them the Kingdom, but, the sinfulness of man betrayed this cause, and, as far as man was concerned, smashed all hope by crucifying Jesus upon the Cross. But the mercy and grace of God made the very death of Christ the means of "making things right." Christ became the very sacrificial lamb which once and for all paid the price of Adam's sin (which had been inherited by all mankind) for all eternity by dying upon the Cross the very day that Passover lambs were being slaughtered. Some like to blame the death of Christ on the Jewish people, but they are wrong in doing so. Every person in the world was responsible for causing Christ to go to the Cross, for we were all under the curse of Adam's sin—and we are all sinners. Besides, no power in the universe could have taken the life of Jesus if he had not allowed it to be so. *"...I lay down my life, that I might take it again. No man taketh it from me, but I lay it down of myself. I have power to lay it down, and I have power to take it again..."* **(John 10:17-18).**

Another symbolic lesson seems to lie in the relationship existing between the sacred year and the civil year. The sacred year begins with the month Nisan, which roughly corresponds with our month April. The civil year begins with the month Tishri, roughly corresponding with the month of October. If the two systems were placed side by side, their concurrent months would align as demonstrated in **Chart 2.**

CHART 2
ALIGNMENT OF THE SACRED AND CIVIL YEAR MONTHS IN THE JEWISH CALENDAR

1	2	3	4	5	6	7	8	9	10	11	12	(Sacred Year)			
			(Civil Year)	1	2	3	4	5	6	7	8	9	10	11	12

The Jewish Sacred Year and Civil Year both contain twelve months. he Sacred Year begins with the month Nisan (April), and ends with the month Adar (March). The Civil Year begins with Tishri (October), and ends with Elul (September). The two systems align as shown in the diagram, the 1st month of the Civil Year corresponding with the 7th month of the Sacred Year, etc. Even though the Jewish New Year is celebrated in the Fall, the months are designated by the numbers contained in the Sacred Year.

If the fourteen days of the Great Two Weeks are laid out in a single line numbering one through fourteen, and if the Eight Days of Man, which reach from the beginning of the seventh day of the Creative

Week on through the seven following Great Days to the end of the Millennial Kingdom, are arranged beside the Great Two Weeks in the same manner in which they fall in history, it is apparent that their concurrent days show the same numbers as the concurrent months in the sacred and civil years **(See Chart 3)**.

Although the Great Two Weeks contain fourteen days while the sacred and civil year calendars contain only twelve months, we nevertheless receive a remarkable picture of man's history, embodied in the Jewish calendar.

It might be noted here that the Jewish Tabernacle, through the differing measurements of its three main areas, also seems to embody a picture of the Eight Days of Man, even dividing the days into sections denoting the period from the Creation of man to the Messiah, on through the Church Age to the Return of Christ, then, showing the glorious Millennial Kingdom when Christ will reign on earth. This theory is more fully examined in the closing portions of **Chapter 9,** "More Specific Examples of the Signs of the Times."

CHART 3
ALIGNMENT OF THE GREAT TWO WEEKS AND THE EIGHT DAYS OF MAN

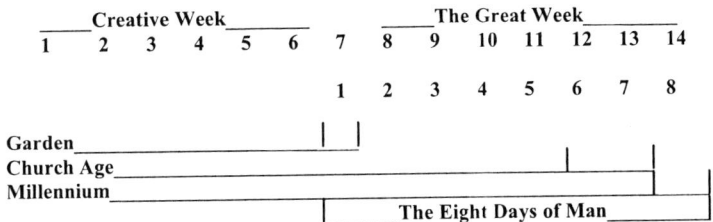

There are fourteen Great Days contained in the Great Two Weeks, composing the Creative Week and the Great Week. The eight Days of Man extend from the time in the Garden of Eden when God retired from Adam and Eve, leaving them on their own during the 7th day of the Creative week, until the close of the Millennium. They align as shown above, the 1st day of the "Eight Days" corresponding with the 7th of the Great Two Weeks, etc.

James F. Webb

Chapter 3
The Promise of the Coming Messiah

"For unto us a child is born, unto us a son is given: and the government shall be upon his shoulder; and his name shall be called Wonderful, Counsellor, The mighty God, The everlasting Father, The Prince of Peace" **(Isaiah 9:6).**

On the night he was born, angels announced the glorious event to humble and lowly shepherds abiding in a field near Bethlehem, watching their flock during the night hours **(Luke 2:8-14).** An unusual star appeared, shinning forth from the firmament of the heavens, directing the wise men from the east to Judea, to the city of his birth, and even to the very spot where the young child was living at the time **(Matthew 2:1-12).** By themselves, these happenings should be enough to convince serious minds that the advent was truly ordained by God.

But these were not the first words or signs concerning the promised Messiah. Prophets had proclaimed his coming from the very first pages of the Written Word of God, and these accounts show plainly that the predictions and oral declarations were well known to men long before Moses penned the first five books of the Bible.

The first spoken prophecy of a Redeemer was directed to the serpent in the Garden of Eden, but was made in the presence of Adam and Eve.

"And I will put enmity between thee and the woman, and between thy seed and her seed; it shall bruise thy head, and thou shalt bruise his heel" **(Genesis 3:15).**

An even earlier prophecy of Christ is recorded in God's Written Word. It is not a "spoken" prophecy, but is contained within the actions surrounding one of God's creative works. In **I Corinthians 15:45-47,** Jesus Christ is referred to as the last or Second Adam. God caused a deep sleep to fall upon the first Adam, opened his side, removed a rib, and created Eve, who would become his bride **(Genesis 2:21-22).** By the will of God, a deep sleep (death) fell also upon the

Second Adam as he hung upon the Cross. His side was pierced by a Roman spear, and his bride, the Church, was purchased by the blood that he shed there **(Colossians 1:14)**. That the Church is the bride of Christ is plainly made manifest in the Bible **(Matthew 9:15)**. In **Ephesians 5:25-32.** husbands are admonished to love their wives even as Christ also loved the Church, and gave himself for it. Men are further instructed to love their wives as though they were their own bodies, for this is the purpose of marriage, that two shall become one. Verse thirty-two clearly states that Paul is speaking of Christ and the Church. The Church, as the espoused bride of Christ, is referred to as the body of Christ **(Ephesians 5:30; Colossians 1:18)**.

John the Baptist, reaffirming his own disciples that he was not the Messiah, made the statement, *"He that hath the bride is the bridegroom"* **(John 3:29)**. This is a definite indication that John believed himself to be neither the bridegroom nor the bride. John lived his life before the Cross, and died while the Dispensation of Law was yet in effect. He could not have become a member of the Church, the body of Christ, until after Christ had given his life upon the hill of Golgotha. Neither can we assume that the bride consists of the Redeemed of all ages, for John was truly among the Redeemed, Christ himself attesting to the fact that there was none greater among men than John **(Matthew 11:11)**. But John referred to himself as the *"friend of the bridegroom,"* and, as such, to be included among the guests at the Marriage Feast of the Lamb.

From the earliest times, there was never any doubt, among those who truly loved the Lord, that, one day the Messiah would come. Adam did not doubt the promise of the *"woman's seed,"* and Abel declared his faith in the future sacrifice of the Lamb of God when he *"brought of the firstlings of his flock"* and offered them to the Lord. Enoch walked with God and believed the promises concerning the Messiah, that he would come, and even proclaimed one of the earliest recorded Biblical prophecies concerning the Second Coming of Jesus **(Jude 14-15)**.

By faith, throughout the pages of the Old Testament, holy men served God, believing his words and promises, and trusting that, in God's own time, the Redeemer would come and settle the long standing and ponderous debt of Sin. Men like Noah, and Abraham, Isaac, Jacob, Joseph, and Moses, Joshua, Samuel, David, Elijah, and Isaiah, Jeremiah, and Daniel were not made righteous because they were good men, or performed admirable works. They were accounted as "righteous" because they placed their confidence and faith in the word of God **(Hebrews 11** and **Romans 4:1-3)**.

The First Coming of Christ was certainly not intended to be a surprise to the world existing around two-thousand years ago. His credentials, enabling all who cared to easily recognize him, had been carefully recorded in the Scriptures, read in the synagogues, and pondered by the most learned men.

MESSIANIC PROPHECIES FROM THE OLD TESTAMENT: a child would be born which would also be called the Son of God given to men **(Isaiah 9:6; Psalm 2:7)**. He would be a descendant of Abraham **(Genesis 12:3)**. It was further designated that he would be a descendant of David **(II Samuel 7:12-16; Psalm 89:3-4; 110:1; 132:11; Isaiah 9:7; 11:1)**. His birth would be miraculous—born of a virgin **(Isaiah 7:14)**. His birth would be in the city of Bethlehem **(Micah 5:2)**. There would be a massacre of children at Bethlehem **(Jeremiah 31:15)**.

He would dwell for a while in Egypt, then would be called forth from that land **(Hosea 11:1)**. He would grow up in the province of Galilee **(Isaiah 9:1-2)**, and Nazareth would be his hometown **(Matthew 2:23; Isaiah 11:1)**. An Elijah-like herald would immediately precede him **(Isaiah 40:3-5; Malachi 3:1; 4:5-6)**. He would have a ministry of healing **(Matthew 8:17; Isaiah 53:4)**, and would employ parables in teaching **(Isaiah 6:9-10; Psalm 78:2)**. He would make a grand entry into Jerusalem, riding upon an ass **(Zechariah 9:9)**. He would be betrayed by a friend for thirty pieces of silver **(Zechariah 11:12-13; Psalm 41:9)**. He would be despised and rejected **(Isaiah 53:3)**. He would be led as a lamb to the slaughter, opening not his mouth **(Isaiah 53:7-8)**. He would die for the sins of men **(Isaiah 53:5,6,8, & 12)**. He would die among transgressors **(Isaiah 53:9 & 12),** and would be buried by the rich **(Isaiah 53:9)**. He would be given gall and vinegar **(Psalm 69:21)**. He would be mocked while hanging upon the Cross **(Psalm 22:7-8)**. His hands and his feet would be pierced **(Psalm 22:16)**. Lots would be cast for his garments **(Psalm 22:18)**. Not one of his bones would be broken **(Numbers 9:12; Psalm 34:20)**. He would rise from the grave on the third day **(Psalm 16:9-10; Matthew 12:40; Jonah 1:17)**. His bride, the Church, would be composed mainly of Gentiles **(Psalms 2:8; 22:27)**. And these are but a small percentage of the galaxy of signs, prophecies, types and antitypes, and numerous predictions contained within Old Testament Scripture.

THE SEVENTY WEEKS OF DANIEL: Probably, to the average church member, Daniel is best remembered as the man who was cast into a lion's den because of his faith in the true God of Israel. He is also known as a prophet who was shown several things pertaining to the last days and the Second Return of Christ to the world. Less known to most people is the prophecy of the Seventy Weeks, but it remains one of the most remarkable and accurate forecasts of the Savior's first appearance as a man upon the earth.

"Seventy weeks are determined upon thy people and upon thy holy city, to finish the transgression, and to make an end of sins, and to make reconciliation for iniquity, and to bring in everlasting righteousness, and to seal up the vision and prophecy, and to anoint the most Holy. Know therefore and understand, that from the going forth of the commandment to restore and to build Jerusalem unto the Messiah the Prince shall be seven weeks, and threescore and two weeks: the street shall be built again, and the wall, even in troublous times. And after threescore and two weeks shall Messiah be cut off, but not for himself" **(Daniel 9:24-26a).**

The verses quoted above are disputed by some who wish to play down Bible prophecy, who infer that the predictions, attributed to the words of an angel to Daniel, are actually the product of a much later time, being written and inserted into Scripture after the events described had already occurred. But though some may try to challenge and dispute the teachings of this prophecy, it still remains a well founded, authoritative announcement establishing the time of the Messiah's redemptive visit. It is commonly referred to as "Daniel's Seventy Weeks."

The events related in the Book of Daniel fall within a period of time known as the "Seventy-Year Exile." In B.C. 606, the Babylonian king, Nebuchadnezzar, besieged and took the city of Jerusalem. Many Jews were at this time forcibly extracted from their land and carried away to the area of Babylon. Daniel, who was a young man, was among those transported into captivity.

The captivity was to last for seventy years, according to prophecy, and if it began in B.C. 606, it was to end in B.C. 536. It is estimated that Daniel achieved understanding of this fact during the sixty-eighth year of the exile, which was the first year of the reign of the Persian king, Darius **(Daniel 9:1),** and that this understanding was obtained by reading the book of the prophet Jeremiah. The verses explaining the Seventy-Year Exile are found in **Jeremiah 25:11-12.** Daniel's Seventy Weeks should not be confused with the seventy years of the Exile.

While in deep prayer, petitioning the Lord to forgive the sins of Israel and to truly bring to pass the termination of the years of captivity, Daniel was visited by the angel Gabriel, who unfolded to him the details of the Seventy Weeks. The end of the Jewish Exile was indeed very near at hand, but the close of the seventy-year period would, in itself, bring other events to pass which would eventually permit an accurate determination of the time that the Messiah would come. When the seventy years had been accomplished, Jewish people did return to Jerusalem, and set up an altar to the Lord and repaired dwellings in which to live. The city was not truly restored until a later date.

"Know therefore and understand, that from the going forth of the commandment to restore and to build Jerusalem unto the Messiah the Prince shall be seven weeks, and threescore and two weeks" **(Daniel 9:25a).**

The event from which the seventy weeks were to be counted was *"the going forth of the commandment to restore and to build Jerusalem."* Although the Bible records three decrees concerning the city of Jerusalem, only the commandment by Artaxerxes, king of Persia, actually directs the reconstruction of the city. The story is told in **Nehemiah 2:1-8.**

According to the prophecy of the Seventy Weeks, from the above commandment to rebuild the city of Jerusalem until the coming of the Messiah would be a period of time designated to Daniel as sixty-nine weeks. Theologians inform us that the literal language used in this instance does not imply a week of seven 24-hour days, but a week of years, or seventy weeks with each week made up of seven years. Therefore, the angel Gabriel advised Daniel that from the commandment to restore the city of Jerusalem to the coming of the Messiah would be a period of 483 years.

Unfortunately, modern ability to estimate and fix dates in certain areas of history, cannot supply an exact number for the year in which Artaxerxes issued his commandment, other than that it was in the month of Nissan (April) in the twentieth year of the king's reign. Ussher estimates the year as B.C. 454. If we count ahead 483 years from this date we are brought to A.D. 30, the year Christ rode into Jerusalem on April 2, offering himself as the Messiah. He was crucified later in that week.

"And after threescore and two weeks shall Messiah be cut off, but not for himself" **(Daniel 9:26a).**

However, it should be said that there are Bible scholars who suggest that the Seventy weeks are not to be counted in Gregorian years, but in "Prophetic Years" (a prophetic year is believed to have 360 days, or, twelve months of 30 days each). By this method, the sixty-nine weeks would add up to just over 476 Gregorian years, and would place the date of Artaxerxes' commandment in the first part of B.C. 447, unless, of course, by the coming of the Messiah was actually meant the beginning of his ministry. This would possibly place the decree of Artaxerxes about three to four years earlier, moving the date back to B.C. 450 or 451. To be perfectly honest, I confess I sometimes have doubts concerning the prophetic year of 360 days. I believe it is based on the account of the Flood found in Genesis. But we have already discussed that we do not know which calendar Mosses actually used (the Egyptian calendar of twelve months of 30 days each, with 5 days added at the end, or, another calendar).

Much serious study had been undertaken by many students of the Bible attempting to resolve the issue, and to determine the correct date of the Persian king's order, but it would seem that we live too far this side of the time of Artaxerxes, and history is too dim concerning the occasion. However, those who lived in the years before and during the First Advent of Christ were much closer to the scene, and the Jewish people of the time took great pride in keeping family records throughout their generations. The coming of the Messiah should have been recognized by far more than just a few. But, one thing is certain to those who hold the Bible as the inspired Word of God. Whether the Seventy Weeks of Daniel were counted in Gregorian years, Prophetic years, or any other type of years, the prophecy given to Daniel certainly does point to the time of the ministry of Jesus, and is extraordinary in its accuracy. The seventieth week of this prophecy still awaits fulfillment, but will be accomplished in the seven years of the Tribulation Period.

James F. Webb

Chapter 4
The Birth and Early Years of Jesus

"And she brought forth her firstborn son, and wrapped him in swaddling clothes, and laid him in a manger; because there was no room for him in the inn" **(Luke 2:7).**

The Jewish nation had long awaited the coming of Messiah (the Anointed One), and never so anxiously as during those early years of the Roman occupancy. The armies of the Roman Empire, long recognized as a formidable force, extended its iron-like grasp into the Eastern Mediterranean countries during what our present age refers to as the first century before Christ. In B.C. 63, Roman general Gnaeus Pompeus Magnus (Pompey) laid siege to a Jewish force within the Temple walls at Jerusalem. The siege lasted for three months until the Roman soldiers finally succeeded in breaching the fortress. It is reported that Pompey took advantage of the Jewish laws of the Sabbath, erecting his machines and performing other preparations for battle while the Jews were forbidden to commit any act of war, except to defend themselves against direct attack. The Temple was taken upon a Sabbath, and priests were slain while in the very act of performing the ritual duties and sacrifices at the altar. In all, it is estimated that 12,000 Jews lost their lives upon that day.

It was also upon that day that Pompey committed an act which was strictly outlawed by Jewish law. He entered the most Holy of Holies, a thing allowed only to a specially chosen and prepared priest in the performance of a very special ceremony. According to the Jewish historian, Josephus, this vile and profaning act occurred upon the 23rd day of Silvan (June). It is reported that he found the room empty—the Ark of the covenant apparently moved to another location.

It did not follow that Pompey's victory brought peace to the Holy Land. The problems of Rome's internal struggles at the time only united to keep the area in a state of constant turmoil. The generals of Rome vied one against another, using Jewish terrain for many of their greedy battles over power and authority. Julius Caesar was victorious over Pompey and attempted to restore some semblance of order to the land, but his assassination in B.C. 44, disrupted the fragile situation. More power struggles followed, eventually placing Herod the Great in power under Roman authority.

An Idumean by birth, Herod was not considered a real Jew, although, many years in the past, the subjects of Idumea had been conquered by John Hyrcanus during the period of the Maccabees, and were forced to submit to circumcision and adoption into the Jewish religion.

Herod's skill in balancing the opposing factors within his territory was admirable, but at times his rule was harsh and cruel. Upon coming to the throne, he ordered hundreds to be put to death among those who had sided against him. There were also numerous family problems and the executions of several sons and a wife, causing Caesar Augustus to comment, "It is better to be Herod's pig than his son."

"And it came to pass in those days, that there went out a decree from Caesar Augustus, that all the world should be taxed (and this taxing was first made when Cyrenius was governor of Syria). And all went to be taxed, every one to his own city. And Joseph also went up from Galilee, out of the city of Nazareth, into Judea, unto the city of David, which is called Bethlehem; (because he was of the house and lineage of David:) To be taxed with Mary his espoused wife, being great with child" **(Luke 2:1-5).**

In the past, there has been a degree of confusion concerning the time of this particular taxation. Cyrenius is the Greek form of the last name of Publius Sulpicius Quirinius, a former Roman senator who was placed in charge of Syria and the land of the Jews. It would therefore seem that he was the Roman authority over Herod. A census was known to have been carried out under him in about A.D. 6, but this would have been too late to be the census spoken of by Luke. However, information has been found implying that Quirinius was twice the governor of Syria, the first time falling at a point in history completely in agreement with the account given in the **Gospel of Luke.**

Mary was with child as she accompanied Joseph on the journey from Nazareth of Galilee to Bethlehem, which was located about five miles south of Jerusalem. Roads were not super highways in that age, nor did people travel in comfortable automobiles, so the trip would have been particularly difficult for her. When they arrived in the town of David's birth, they found crowded streets and the inn already overloaded. The inn of Bethlehem (inns if more than one existed) was usually filled with many travelers, for the city was located along the great ridge road running from north to south, from Galilee and beyond to Egypt in the south. The taxation also must have added to the crowd of people present in that location, as those descended from David were required to travel there. The Bible tells us that the couple found no lodging in the city, but, apparently, some concerned person directed them to the stable where Jesus was actually born.

Both Mary and Joseph were aware that the child she gave birth to shortly after arriving in Bethlehem was a child directly sent by the hand of the Lord. At least nine months before, the angel Gabriel had visited Mary, and announced that she would be with child by the Holy Ghost, and further instructed her that they should name the child Jesus.

"He shall be great, and shall be called the Son of the Highest: and the Lord God shall give unto him the throne of his father David: And he shall reign over the house of Jacob for ever; and of his kingdom there shall be no end" **(Luke 1:32-33).**

Luke also tells us of the angelic visit to the shepherds, who were watching their flock during the night. The field where they were located was probably the same field, east of the city, where shepherds continue to watch over sheep even to this day. I like to believe that shepherds were very near the heart of God, for Jesus often demonstrated a special place in his heart for those who were shepherds. After all, he was the Good Shepherd, and completely faithful to his cause, eventually laying down his very life for the human sheep of the world!

But it would seem that there were very few people, other than the shepherds and those that the shepherds themselves notified, who actually knew about the new child born in the stable on that particular night.

Luke tells us in chapter two that, on the eighth day after the birth, the child was circumcised according to Jewish law. Then, after the forty days required for the purification of a woman who had just given birth, he was taken to the temple in Jerusalem where a special offering was made. The fact that the parents of Jesus offered a pair of turtledoves, or two young pigeons **(Luke 2:24)**, seems to suggest that the couple were poor.

The young baby Jesus did not go without notice in the temple, although the temple priests, who should have known the prophecies of the Messiah and should have been looking for him, saw only a young mother and father with their recently born child. Instead, it was an elderly man and woman who recognized the child for whom he actually was. Elderly Simeon and Anna blessed the infant and prophesied concerning the glory of his future.

We do not know exactly how long Joseph and Mary remained in Bethlehem with their son, Jesus, but another happening described in the Bible does imply they may have tarried there for some time. Matthew tells of the visit of the Magi (Wise Men), who had witnessed a new star in the sky from their land to the east, and had interpreted the celestial object as the birth of a great king in Israel. Seeking a child of royalty, they went first to Jerusalem and sought out Herod. Here they learned of the Messianic prophecy that Messiah would be born in Bethlehem. They were soon on the short journey to the town of David, but not before Herod had petitioned them to go find the child, then return to tell him where the child lived that he might go also and worship him. The wise men found the family of Jesus no longer living in a manger but in a house, and he was no longer a baby, but a young child. The wise men offered their gifts, then, warned in a dream that they should not go back to Herod, they departed to their own country another way. Joseph, also being warned in a dream of Herod's intentions to destroy the child, did as the angel in the dream had advised, and immediately took his family to the safety of Egypt.

Herod soon realized that the Wise Men did not intend to come back to reveal the location of the child, so he sought to take matters into his own hands. He ordered the slaughter of all children in Bethlehem who fell into a certain age bracket—two years old and younger. When he set the age below which to slay the children, he did so in accordance with the period of time having elapsed since the Wise Men first saw the star in the east. Since the age was set at two years, and the fact that Herod would probably have given himself a margin of at least three to six months in order to be sure he had slain the young child, we can assume that Christ may have been as much as one and a half years old when the Magi came.

The modern calendar was created to be counted from the birth of Christ, but, the original calculations were a little off. It is now known that Herod the Great died either in the last part of March or the first part of April in B.C. 4. We know the time of his death because of the writings of the Jewish historian, Josephus, who associates the death of the king with a certain eclipse of the moon. Modern scientists know that eclipse occurred on March 13, B.C. 4. Estimates made on these facts tell us that Christ may have actually been born somewhere between the fall season of B.C. 6, and the spring of B.C. 5.

Unless a date of importance is recorded at the time of its happening by some authoritative source, it is usually extremely difficult to estimate its exact point in history after the elapse of a large span of time. This is particularly true after several centuries.

In the year, A.D. 526, the Emperor Justinian requested the monk Dionysius Exigus to perfect a new calendar, counting from the Birth of Christ. Time had long been determined in the Roman Empire by counting the years from the date of the founding of the city of Rome. The new Christian calendar would take the place of the Roman calendar.

When making his calculations, Dionysius "estimated" that the Birth of Christ had occurred in the 753rd year of the Empire of Rome, which date was later found to be in error. The Gregorian calendar, used today, determines its years from the original calculations of Dionysius, even though it has now been accepted that the actual Birth of Christ took place at least four to six years earlier. I do not know the methods used by Dionysius to affix the Birth of Christ, but it is now known he was in error.

After the death of Herod, Joseph's family returned from Egypt, but, learning that the son of Herod the great reigned in his place, they bypassed Judea and retuned to the city of Nazareth in Galilee.

Luke is the only Gospel that tells us anything concerning the childhood of Jesus, the other three Gospels going straight to the ministry of John the Baptist. But that which we receive from the beloved physician is very scant. In **Luke 2:40,** we are told simply that *"the child grew, and waxed strong in the spirit, filled with wisdom and the grace of God was upon him."* The same chapter also relates the trip to Jerusalem when Jesus was twelve years old, when he tarried behind the others to visit with the wisest men of the temple and astonished them with his understanding and answers.

Luke tells us that he was subject to his parents, Joseph and Mary, that Mary, like most devoted mothers would have, kept the sayings and events of Jesus in her heart. The author of the third gospel also tells us that "Jesus increased in wisdom and stature, and in favor with God and man" **(Luke 2:52).**

The Bible tells us little more than these things concerning the childhood of Jesus. The Bible does make us aware that Joseph, his father, was a carpenter. We are also told that Jesus was not an only child, for others are mentioned in **Matthew 13:55-56.** But, if he was not the only child that Mary gave birth to, he was the first, and the only one who was the **Son of God!**

Chapter 5
The Earthly Ministry of Christ

"The Spirit of the Lord is upon me, because he hath anointed me to preach the Gospel to the poor; he hath sent me to heal the brokenhearted, to preach deliverance to the captive, and recovering of sight to the blind, to set at liberty them that are bruised, to preach the acceptable year of the Lord" **(Luke 4:18-10).**

Luke informs us that John the Baptist began his ministry in the fifteenth year of the reign of Tiberius Caesar. We are also told that Pontius Pilate was the governor of Judea, Herod was the tetrarch of Galilee, while Phillip, brother of Herod, ruled over Iturea and Trachonia (both territories located across the Jordan River, north and east of the Lake of Galilee). Luke further tells us that Lysanias was tetrarch of Abilene (an area of land north of Iturea), and Annas and Caiaphas were the high priests. Actually, there was only one high priest, but, Annas, the father-in-law of Caiaphas, had been high priest at an earlier time and two of his sons had held the office prior to Caiaphas. The position of high priest, once considered a very referent and holy office, was now chosen and appointed by the foreign government of Rome. Even the special clothing worn by the high priest during certain occasions and feast days was held and kept in the Antonia fortress, located adjacent to the temple and under the care of Roman soldiers. Apparently, Annas, at least ten years after he had held the office of high priest, still possessed such sway over those in the temple, and over his son-in-law, that most of the Jewish populace considered him to share the position with Caiaphas.

Today, it is generally accepted that John the Baptist began his public ministry in A.D. 26, and that the author of the third Gospel counts the fifteen years from the year A.D. 12, when it is thought that Tiberius became co-regent with Augustus. Tiberius succeeded to sole regent in A.D. 14. Luke also informs us that John the Baptist was actually a second cousin to Jesus, but we are not told that John and Jesus ever met except as unborn babies when Mary went to visit her cousin, Elizabeth, the mother of John the Baptist. However, there seems to be little doubt that John knew exactly who Jesus was when he approached him at the Jordan River, for he proclaimed that he needed to be baptized of Jesus and not Jesus of him. In the first chapter of John, John the Baptist declares that he knew the identity of Jesus when he saw him, because the Spirit of God descended from Heaven like a dove, and abided upon him.

Some think John to have been a member of a group called the Essenes, an almost monastic community of people living in the desert south of Jericho and near the Dead Sea. However, his mode of dress does not seem to compare with the Essenes, nor does his bold public preaching that the Messiah was at hand. But he did live in the desert area (the wilderness between Jerusalem and the Jordan), and he baptized in the Jordan River at a spot not far from the ancient city of Jericho. He was executed by the order of Herod Antipas for directly speaking out against the unlawful wedding of the tetrarch to Herodias, while she was still married to his brother Philip. But this happened after he had proclaimed Jesus as the Lamb of god and had performed his baptism.

It is certain that the Jewish generation of that time had not seen a man who preached with the power of John the Baptist. Many insisted that he had to be some "great one" in order to wield his messages in a manner so effective that it stirred multitudes. They questioned him as to whether he was the Messiah (Christ) or perhaps Elijah. He assured them that he was not, but did declare that he was *"the voice of one crying in the wilderness,"* as **Isaiah** had prophesied.

At a later time, after John had been seized and imprisoned by Herod Antipas, Jesus praised him before a multitude of people, saying, *"For this is he, of whom it is written, Behold, I send my messenger before thy face, which shall prepare thy way before thee. Verily I say unto you, among them that are born of women there hath not risen a greater than John the Baptist."* He then continued to tell them that, referring to the prophecy that Elijah would come to prepare the way for the Messiah, if the nation of Israel would receive him (Jesus) for who he actually was (the true Messiah), then John the Baptist would have been the real Elijah. But, God, knowing by his foreknowledge, that Jesus Christ would be rejected at that time, sent John, an Elijah-like preacher and a truly great man in himself.

After his baptism, Jesus was led by the Spirit into the wilderness, where he endured a lengthy time of fasting and testing. During these forty days, Satan used all of his wiles in a vain attempt to persuade Jesus to forsake his mission on earth. The three temptations he used actually compare with **I John 2:16,** where the apostle categorizes the temptations of the world as the lust of the flesh, the lust of the eyes, and the pride of life. It is probably true that these same three desires prompted Satan in his original rebellion against God, as well as tempting Adam and Eve in the Garden of Eden.

When the forty days were ended, Jesus apparently returned to the area of the Jordan near the spot where John the Baptist held his services. The preacher, clothed in his raiment of camel's hair and leathern girdle, observed Jesus walking and pointed him out to two of his own disciples who stood near him, and declared, *"Behold the Lamb of God!"* The two disciples followed after Jesus, and probably remained with him into the evening.

The Bible directly tells us that one of the two was Andrew, the brother of Simon Peter. the other is believed to be John the apostle. The story is told in the first chapter of the **Gospel of John,** but the Apostle never seems to mention his own name in his own work, although it is noted quite well in the other gospels. John does point out one fact in the last chapter of his Gospel. Once more, he mentions without name the disciple he has anonymously referred to throughout his writing, but this time follows his words by making the statement, "This is the disciple which testifieth of these things, and wrote these things." We can only suppose that John modestly refused to direct excessive attention to himself.

They were not with Jesus long until they were so impressed that they soon became the first disciples of Christ. The following day Andrew went to find his brother Simon Peter, and soon ushered him into the presence of the one to whom, for the rest of their lives, they would wholeheartedly dedicate their faith while spreading the jubilant news of God's salvation throughout the world.

The first miracle Jesus performed was at the wedding in Cana, a small village to the north of Nazareth. It was there that he changed the water into wine when the original supply had been consumed. The Bible does mention that disciples of Christ were present at that wedding but their names or number are not given.

His miracles were not limited to the one performed at the wedding in Cana, for he began to show his ability to heal those who were sick and stricken with differing types of very serious afflictions, considered beyond healing in the first century. In fact, even the amazing medical knowledge of the modern world must still admit it cannot cure those suffering under the grasp of many of the serious ailments Christ banished in a moment.

At the beginning of his ministry, Jesus echoed the message of John the Baptist, that the long-awaited Messiah had come, and the Kingdom was now at hand. He repeated John's message because it was true. Jesus was the Messiah, and, if the nation of Israel would accept him for who he actually was, the Kingdom would then come into being. It was an honest offer on the part of God. But, his foreknowledge knew it would not come to pass at that time, but he performed enough signs and miracles to support the facts and prove his identity—if the hearts of men had only listened.

I do not know the exact length of time that transpired until Jesus stood in the synagogue in Nazareth and officially announced to those of his home town that he was the Messiah. He read from **Isaiah 61:1,** where it says *"The Spirit of the Lord is upon me to preach the Gospel to the poor; he hath sent me to heal the broken-hearted, to preach deliverance to the captives, and recovering of sight to the blind, to set at liberty them that are bruised, to preach the acceptable year of the Lord"* **(Luke 4:18-19).** He at that point genuinely offered himself as the "anointed one" they had waited for, but their reaction matched the reaction of most of the rest of Israel at that time—they rejected him. His message soon changed to the good news still proclaimed by his followers even today, that man may be reunited with God and fine salvation through the sacrifice and blood of Christ (Messiah) upon the Cross of Golgotha.

The Bible does not tell us the details of the calling of *"all"* of the twelve apostles, nor at what exact time in the ministry of Jesus they were called. We do know that in the **sixth chapter of John** they apparently had been selected, for they were referred to in **verse 67** as "the twelve."

They were a varied sort of men, chosen from differing levels and vocations. At least four were fishermen: Peter, Andrew, James and John. They were in partnership with the father of James and John, Zebedee. Perhaps there were other sons of Zeberdee which helped carry on the family business after the four left to walk after Jesus. There is an indication that at least some boatmen were hired by Zeberdee to carry on what must have been a sizable fishing endeavor (the Bible does mention several other boats involved in relation to those manned by James, John, Peter, and Andrew).

Phillip was called early in the ministry of Christ, and, Phillip quickly sought out his brother, Nathaniel. In the lists of the twelve given in the Bible, Nathaniel's name is not mentioned, but, some theologians believe he is the same person as Bartholomew, Bartholomew being the surname of Nathaniel, as was Bar-Jona the surname of Peter (Peter's original name was Simon until Jesus changed it to Peter).

Matthew was a publican (a tax collector) called somewhat later than the first six. He left a very prosperous business to walk the roads with Jesus, but was richer by far because of that choice. James, the son of Alphaeus, is thought to be by some the same person elsewhere referred to as James the Less. After the Cross, he remained in Jerusalem and became the leader of that church. He was also known as the Lord's brother, but it is not entirely clear that he was a true brother as we use the term, today. In New Testament times, the term "brother" often meant a "close relative." Many think he may actually have been a cousin.

Of Simon the Canaanite **(Matthew 10:4 & Mark 3:18),** also called Simon Zelotes, little is known. Canaanite was actually from a Aramaic word which meant Zealot. Some believe he may have been a member of a band of patriots, or Jewish zealots who resisted Roman rule.

Judas the son of James **(Luke 6:16)** is thought to be the Thaddeus of Matthew and Mark. It is suspected he was referred to by another name than Judas to identify him from Judas Iscariot. John, when he refers to him by Judas, quickly adds the explanation, "not Iscariot."

Judas Iscariot, if the name, Iscariot, as some believe, does mean "man of Kerioth," may have been the only one of the twelve who was not from Galilee. He was entrusted with the purse, which contained whatever money the group may have possessed. Offended when Christ rebuked him for his criticism concerning the anointing of oil by Mary, the sister of Martha and Lazarus, Judas went to the temple priests and planned the betrayal.

In the beginning of his ministry, Jesus copied the message of John the Baptist. He did so for a very specific reason. John the Baptist had appeared out of the wilderness east of Jerusalem, proclaiming that the Messiah, the long-awaited deliverer and anointed one of God was truly about to come at last. Jesus knew that the expectant hopes of the people would be lifted to an elevated height. The "deliverer" had been promised even from the first days after Eden, and the desire in the hearts of the Jewish citizens, now, under the foot of Rome, especially longed for the prophecies to come true. From the few accounts of the early life of Christ, we can see that he was completely aware of his mission to earth even at the quite young age of twelve, when he confounded the nation's most learned men as he stood in the temple at Jerusalem. When his parents found him and questioned him, he replied, *"Know ye not that I must be about my father's business?"*

In the early part of his ministry, his message announced that the kingdom and the Messiah were at hand. This was the message John the Baptist had proclaimed, and **it was true!** The Messiah had come into the world, and, if Israel "had" accepted him, the kingdom would have been established at that time. The Lord had made a legitimate offer to his chosen people, but, just as he had known beforehand that it would be, the offer was soundly rejected. Even those of his own village including many of his close kinsmen refuted his claims, turning violently upon him after he read to them the words from **Isaiah 61:1,** then announced that *"this day is this Scripture fulfilled in your ears."*

Jesus was not surprised when he encountered opposition from the very source that should have given him the most support. When whispers began to circulate about his miracles and the words which he spoke, the curiosity of the temple authorities was aroused. They saw only a troublesome Galilean (a territory which had, in the past, created serious problems with the Roman occupational forces, resulting in severe reprisals afflicted upon the Jewish nation), and they attempted to find ways to silence his ministry before it attracted attention and brought more wrath from Roman rulers.

Jesus was aware of the following his own preaching would soon produce, for John had first prophesied his arrival, then singles him out of the many being baptized, and declared him to be the *"Lamb of God, which taketh away the sin of the world."* John had performed no miracles in contrast to the many miracles of Jesus, which only heightened the excitement surrounding the remarkable Galilean. There were many people who listened to the beautiful words of Christ and seriously believed them. But there were others who did not want to love their brothers—at least, they did not want to love Romans. Jesus knew that most of the public flocking to him would rejoice and continue to increase until they learned that he did not intend to lead the nation in an uprising against Rome. Many forsook him at that point.

The inhabitants of Israel, during the ministry of Christ, had grown up under bondage to the Roman Empire. The great patriotic passion within the hearts of those people created a huge longing within them. The overbearing thought on their minds cried out instinctively to once more be free. We should not be quick to judge them because they were blinded to the real reason for the Messiah's coming. They felt their physical pain more than they sensed their need of a Savior who would provide a way to have all their sins forgiven once and for all, and to be truly united with God. But, nevertheless, the message of the Messiah was a legitimate offer. He was the Messiah! His nation just did not understand the reason that Messiah would come.

In the garden, Adam and Eve, the population of the world at that time, had fallen away from God their master. The separation caused by their sin brought with it the penalty of pain, sorrow, heartache, misery, hardship, more sin, aggression, war, hatred, and eventual death, followed by eternal punishment and banishment from the presence of the Lord—**if something were not done to alter that situation.** The Messiah (just as pictured by sacrifices made in temple worship), by the laying down of his own life (the perfect sacrificial lamb sent by God), would provide and make possible a way for men to have their sin forgiven once and for all—for eternity. Simply stated, Adam's sin in the garden was passed along to his children and on to all mankind—for all are the descendants of Adam. The apostle Paul points out that by one man sin entered into the world and all were condemned. He also tells us that by one "perfect" man, Jesus, who, by his virgin birth did not inherit the curse of Adam's sin (that curse being passed through the man to the child), was qualified to forever pay the price of sin. Simply stated, in the Garden of Eden, when Adam disobeyed the Lord and sin entered into the world, the reason for the Messiah to come was to restore man's original fellowship with God! But the misery in Jewish hearts at that time blinded his people, and most turned away from him after they understood he did not intend to lead a military revolt against Rome.

Not all were deaf to his true message, for there were those who remained true to him, and, there were even thousands of Jewish people, including many priests who worked in the Jerusalem temple, who, after his return to heaven, accepted him as their Savior.

His ministry was exercised in the eyes of the public most of the time, but he did increase his private time with his twelve apostles, and, possibly, certain other disciples including several women. Aware from the start what his real mission to earth was really about, he desired to teach a small group of hand-picked men the things they would have to know in order to carry on the work of spreading his message of salvation throughout the whole world. He was aware of the hatred radiating from the office of high priest in Jerusalem. He knew that Annas and Caiaphas, along with their accomplices, were already plotting his death, but Jesus did not allow them the opportunity to carry out their wish until the right time—the week of Passover in A.D. 30.

With the exceptions of certain feast days, Jesus is believed to have spent the larger portion of the years, A.D. 28, and A.D. 29, in the northern province of Galilee. The few times he did visit Jerusalem were enough to nourish the resentment of his many enemies in high places, and, if he had lingered in their vicinity too long, he knew they would surely have made attempts upon his life much earlier than the actual date of the crucifixion.

When the special time planned for the instruction of his chosen apostles had been completed, he led his followers once more to Judea. The scene had been prepared a few days earlier by the sad announcement that Lazarus, the brother of Martha and Mary, had died in Bethany. Jesus delayed his arrival until the corpse had lain in the tomb for four days. This was long enough for effects of deterioration to have began, and a point seemingly beyond the ability of even Jesus to call the poor man back from beyond. But the Savior did call him back, simply by crying out, *"Lazarus, come forth!"* It was a call that reached beyond the tomb, even to the unknown depths of the Bosom of Abraham, and the parted soul of Lazarus returned to his body, and the revived body blossomed forth in renewed health and came forth from the tomb.

When we realize the true identity of Jesus, we understand that the resurrection of the brother of Martha and Mary was but a small thing to the Son of God, and it encourages us with faith, that, one beautiful day, he will cry out once more and all those who sleep in the Lord will come forth to everlasting life. But it amazed those who witnessed the event on that day, and the shock wave of what happened thundered into all the area about Bethany, reaching quite quickly the short distance to Jerusalem, and to the temple.

The twelfth chapter of John tells us that the priests not only sought to put Jesus to death, but Lazarus, also, for many people believed on Jesus because he had raised the man from the dead. Since no further mention is made of the plot against the life of Lazarus, we may assume that the chief priests abandoned the plan, after the crucifixion and resurrection of Jesus from the tomb on Sunday morning. The return of Christ to the world of the living regulated any scheme upon the life of Lazarus a meaningless gesture.

Jesus Christ, the Son of God, came into the world to be the supreme sacrifice that would forever, once and for all, pay the price of sin for every man who ever lived, from Adam and Eve to the last human being to be born into the future of this world. He was the true sacrifice that the Passover lamb pictured. But, it could not be that the "Passover lamb" be slain before the preparation day, when lambs throughout Jerusalem were put to death in readiness for the feast that evening. So, Jesus withdrew from the area for a time, and readied himself and his followers for what lay ahead.

When he returned to Jerusalem, he did so by passing through Jericho where he healed blind Bartemaeus, and converted Zacchaeus, the publican. On Saturday, his group entered Bethany and spent the night at the home of Martha, Mary, and Lazarus. On Sunday, April 2, he rode into Jerusalem on the back of an ass (April 2, 30 A.D., was Nisan 10 in the Jewish calendar, the very day, according to Jewish law, that the Passover lamb was to be selected and presented. Christ, on that same day, presented himself as the supreme sacrificial lamb to take away the sins of the world).

Crowds of people flocked to him in great celebration; so many people, willing to proclaim him the Messiah and follow him blindly without question into battle against the Romans, but so quick to forsake him when they witnessed him in bonds before Pilate. But the crowds of people, who greeted him as the Messiah, misunderstood the true reason for the Messiah. They were willing to follow him to obtain physical freedom from bondage, but fell away from him when they realized he did not intend to cast out the Romans.

Yet, they were no different than we may have been in their place at that time. Through the ages, men have condemned Jewish people for the crucifixion of Christ, and have inflicted inhuman punishments upon their descendants. But the Jews were no more guilty of his death than the rest of the world. We are all responsible for his death, for we are all sinners! Mankind as a whole caused Christ to go the Cross, and, any race of mankind could very possibly have treated him the same way, and did so when they martyred countless of his preachers and followers down through the ages.

Jesus of Nazareth was the Messiah! His First Coming was not extemporaneous, nor without much planning and careful preparation beforehand. The countless announcements and prophecies in the Bible make this very evident. His miraculous birth in the stable at Bethlehem occurred after meticulous arrangements, and happened at the precise time intended.

"To every thing there is a season, and a time to every purpose under the heaven" **(Ecclesiastes 3:1).**

Jesus Christ is the central theme of the Bible, and also the central theme of all history. Every word, every verse, every chapter, and every book contained within Holy Scripture proclaim him, and direct the attention of the reader toward him.

He was the creator of the world, and, also, its Savior. His might and power declare him to be the master of all, yet, he chose to take upon himself the form of a servant, that he might lay down his life to redeem us from sin. We deserved death, but he gave us life; we deserved justice, but he gave us mercy. His love is beyond all understanding, for we were dirty, rotten, unholy worms, crawling in the filth of our own self-made degradation. Sinful and disobedient, we pursued and fed our own selfish desire for things of the flesh, flinging our rebellious nature into the very face of God. And still…*"while we were yet sinners, Christ died for us"* **(Romans 5:8),** and we *"who were once far off are now made nigh by the blood of Christ"* *(***Ephesians 2:13).**

Without Christ, all the wonders of the Bible have no meaning, the joy of life vanishes, and the hope of eternity dims and fades away. He is the shepherd of life and the guarantee of everlasting security. Without Christ…there is nothing!

> Though I should live through untold years,
> And know the wonders of the world,
> Though sages bowed before my knowledge,
> And God his manuscripts unfurled,
> I could not know a single moment,
> So rich in love, so near my soul,
> As in the hour when Jesus found me,
> And took my hand, and made me whole.
> (The author)

While journeying to Damascus, Paul, being suddenly surrounded by light from heaven, fell to the ground and asked the question, *"Who art thou, Lord?"* The same question is asked by many, today. Who was and is Jesus of Nazareth, portrayed in the New Testament as the Messiah?

The Christ of the New Testament is the Jehovah of the Old Testament. The lowly teacher from Galilee, who walked the dusty roads of the Holy Land with Peter, James, and John, also walked with Adam in the green and fertile pathways of Eden. He walked and talked with Enoch, and warned Noah of the impending judgment of the Flood. The Lord that appeared to Abrham in the plains of Mamre, sat and ate with him, allowed the Patriarch to wash his feet, and told him of the approaching destruction of Sodom and Gomorrah, was the same person that ate the Passover supper with the disciples in the upper room, washed their feet, and informed them them of his imminent crucifixion. It was Christ who spoke to Moses from the burning bush, and on Mount Sinai passed close by the prophet, allowing him to gaze upon the Lord from behind. It was Christ who spoke to the prophets of old, and addressed Job from out of a whirlwind. Jesus made it so clear in many statements if we would only heed.

"Before Abraham was, I am" **(John 8:58).**

"He that hath seen me hath seen the father" **(John 14:9).**

"I and my father are one" **(John 10:30).**

The testimony of other Scripture also supports this truth.

"To the only wise God our Savior" **(Jude 25).**

"In the beginning was the Word, and the Word was with God, and the Word was God. The same was in the beginning with God. All things were made by him; and without him was not any thing made that was made" **(John 1:1-3).**

"And the Word was made flesh, and dwelt among us, (and we beheld his glory, the glory of the only begotten of the Father), full of grace and truth" **(John 1:14).**

"In whom we have redemption through his blood, even the forgiveness of sins: who is the image of the invisible God, the firstborn of every creature: for by him were all things created, that are in heaven, and that are in earth, visible and invisible, whether they be

thrones, or dominions, or principalities, or powers: all things were created by him, and for him: and he is before all things, and by him all things consist. And he is the head of the body, the Church: who is the beginning, the firstborn from the dead; that in all things he might have the preeminence" **(Colossians 1:14-18).**

Jesus Christ is God! And it was God who rode into Jerusalem on April 2, A.D. 30, clothed in the flesh of mortal man. And it was God who strode into the Temple and forcibly drove out those thar sold and bought, and overthrew the tables of the money changes, and the seats of them that sold doves. It was God who lawfully asserted, *"It is written, My house shall be called the house of prayer; but ye have made it a den of thieves."*

It was God who cursed the barren fig tree, and taught the people in the Temple, withstanding the debates of the priests, the Pharisees, and the Sadducees. It was God whom Judas betrayed into the hands of enemies, who stood before Pilate and Herod to be judged, and heard the products of his own creation turn against him, crying out in violent resentment, *"Crucify him, Crucify him!"*

It was God whom men stripped and beat and mocked and cruelly scourged—who bore the humiliation of a crown of thorns, and labored beneath a cross toward the hill of Calvary. At the summit of that hill, man drove nails into the hands of God, and left him hanging alone in bitter agony. When Jesus perished upon the Cross that day, God himself poured out his precious blood, and laid down his sinless life for the redemption of all mankind. But it did not end there, in a lifeless tomb. Three days later, God walked out of that place of dread—because he was God! and hell itself was not strong enough to hold him!

"O give thanks unto the Lord; for he is good: for his mercy endureth for ever" **(Psalm 136:1).**

James F. Webb

Chapter 6
The Day of the Cross

"But he was wounded for our transgressions, he was bruised for our iniquities: the chastisement of our peace was upon him; and with his stripes we are healed" **(Isaiah 53:5).**

"But God forbid that I should glory, save in the cross of our Lord Jesus Christ" **(Galatians 6:14a).**

Crucifixion was a cruel and often lingering way to die. By the time Jesus was born, the Romans had employed it for at least two-hundred years, and probably much longer. In fact, I do not know if the Romans were even the originators of that particular method of executing a person. History does tell us that, by B.C. 196, it was already a popular way to punish those whom Rome wanted to make into examples. In that year, slaves and free workers of Etruria, a province immediately north of Rome, rebelled. They were quickly subdued by Roman legions, and many of them subjected to scourging, and then crucified. It seems that scourging was traditionally inflicted before crucifixion, perhaps to weaken the unfortunate victim and, at least sometimes, to hasten his death. Otherwise, a strong man might survive for a number of days, until the strength of his muscles would finally fail and he would perish, usually by suffocation when the body could no longer support itself enough for the lungs to function normally.

The cross was never intended for Roman citizens, but was used primarily upon subjects of other countries whom the government wished to treat with indignation. Therefore, tradition tells us that the Apostle Paul did not suffer crucifixion, for he was a Roman citizen. Beheading, or a firing squad of archers was the usual fate of executing a citizen.

In the Holy Land, the cross was a regular sight, particularly along the main routes just outside prominent cities. Early in the first century before Christ, Alexander Janneus, a Hellenistic descendant of the Hasmoneans, used the method to rid himself of 800 protesting

Pharisee leaders. This was before Pompey's army officially brought Roman rule to Israel, but the presence of Rome was beginning to make itself felt.

Without doubt, Jesus, probably before his twelfth birthday, had witnessed men hanging upon wooden crosses. Shortly after the death of Herod the Great, Judas of Galilee led a serious uprising. Varus, the Roman governor of Syria, marched into the area, put down the rebellion, and had as many as 2,000 patriots nailed to the cross. Before Christ began his public ministry, crosses were an almost common spectacle in the Holy Land.

It is said that the hill of Calvary, or, Golgotha in the Hebrew language, was a site set aside for executions. Golgotha, which means the "place of a skull," was also known as "crucifixion hill." In many places used for this purpose, the upright beams remained permanently fixed in one spot, awaiting the placement of a crossbeam upon them. If this was the case, the condemned person would have been compelled to carry only the heavy crossbeam to the place of execution, rather than the whole cross. I do not know if this was the situation when Christ went to the Cross.

The traditional day of the Cross is Friday, and this day is probably accepted without much thought by most of the Christian world. But closer inspection of the "Passion Week" seems to grant some leverage in choosing the exact day, therefore, causing some differences of opinion, even among very devout Christian people, concerning the actual day of the week Christ was crucified upon.

Perhaps the principal reason for accepting Friday as the day of the Cross is the fact that the Bible makes it very clear that the following day was a Sabbath. The Gospel of John points out that special care was exercised to make sure that none of those suffering crucifixion would remain upon the crosses on the Sabbath day. To hasten the event of death, the legs were broken so that they might not be able to support the weight of the body. The soldiers carried out this sentence upon the two thieves crucified with Jesus. *"But when they came to Jesus, and saw that he was dead already, they brake not his legs"* **(John 19:33).**

But one of the soldiers, wanting to make certain that Christ was really dead, pierced his side with a spear. Then his body was hastily prepared and laid in a borrowed sepulcher near at hand.

Well-meaning Christians of a later age, aware that the traditional Jewish Sabbath is Saturday, adopted Friday as the day of the Cross. This is why many observe Good Friday services in our modern age. The day of resurrection was Sunday, the first day of the week. The Bible points out that Christ arose from the grave upon the third day, but from afternoon Friday to early morning Sunday is less than two days. To account for this, it is asserted that the days are to be counted as "days or portions of days." Therefore, from afternoon Friday to early morning Sunday is a portion of three different days. Apparently, this particular explanation satisfies most.

But, Jesus himself seems to have given a different possible interpretation to the prophecy of the three days.

"For as Jonas was three days and three nights in the whale's belly; so shall the Son of man be three days and three nights in the heart of the earth" **(Matthew 12:40).**

This verse quite plainly indicates that the period of time was not to be counted in days or portions of days, but in daytime periods and nighttime periods. A Friday Cross date cannot fulfill this prophecy. Only two daytime periods are involved (a portion of Friday and all day Saturday), and only two nighttime periods (Friday evening and Saturday morning, and Saturday evening and Sunday morning). See **Chart 4a.**

But Friday does not have to be the day of the Cross in order for the following day to have been a Sabbath. The regular weekly Sabbath did always occur on Saturday, and did not change. But the special Sabbath days, accompanying the holy feast days, were not restricted to any particular day of the week. The beginning of the Jewish religious year was calculated from the new moon, the Passover being fourteen days later. Since the phases of the moon do not follow exactly the calendars of the earth, the special holy day Sabbaths could occur on any day of the week, therefore, causing some weeks to have two Sabbath days. The week of the Cross seems to have been such a week.

*"The Jews therefore, because it was the preparation, that the bodies should not remain upon the cross on the sabbath day (for that sabbath day was an **high day)"* **(John 19:31).**

Some Bible scholars insist that Christ was crucified on Wednesday instead of Friday. This theory proposes that the three days are counted in exact 24-hour periods of time. However, in order for this opinion to comply with the "sign of Jonas," it is necessary to alter the time of resurrection. The time between a Wednesday Cross and a Sunday morning resurrection totals four daytime periods and four nighttime periods. See **Chart 4b.** This is too long if the "sign of Jonas" is taken literally. Therefore, it is theorized that Christ was placed in the grave just before the sun set on Wednesday, and that he came forth from the grave just before sunset on Saturday. One theorist asserts that the women did not come to the tomb Sunday morning, but rather Saturday evening, immediately after sunset, the end of the Sabbath and the beginning of the new day.

Perhaps the Bible does not make a definite statement concerning the exact time of the Savior's resurrection, but some reasonable implications seem to be offered.

"In the end of the sabbath, as it began to dawn toward the first day of the week, came Mary Magdalene and the other Mary to see the sepulcher" **(Matthew 28:1).**

Behold The Bridegroom Cometh

CHART 4
THE DAY OF THE CROSS

"For as Jonas was three days and three nights in the whale's belly; so shall the Son of man be three days and three nights in the heart of the earth" **Matthew 12:40.**

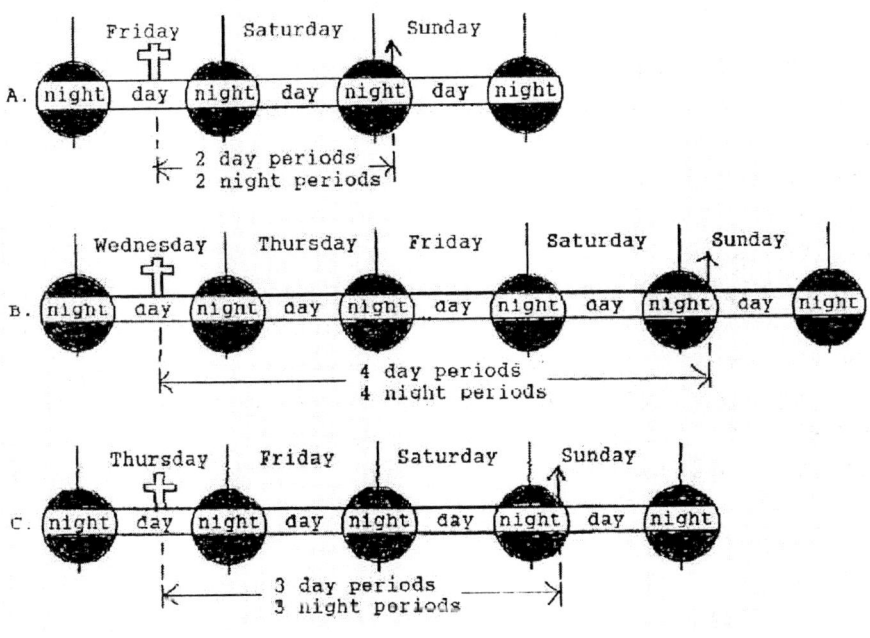

"And when the sabbath was past, Mary Magdalene, and Mary the mother of James, and Salome, had brought sweet spices, that they might come and anoint him. And very early in the morning the first day of the week, they came unto the sepulcher at the rising of the sun" **(Mark 16:1-2).**

"Now upon the first day of the week, very early in the morning, they came unto the sepulcher, bringing the spices which they had prepared, and certain others with them" **(Luke 24:1).**

"The first day of the week cometh Mary Magdalene early, when it was yet dark, unto the sepulcher, and seeth the stone taken away from the sepulcher" **(John 20:1).**

It seems apparent, by mindfully considering the accounts of the four Gospels, that the women did come to the tomb early Sunday morning. All four clearly state that it was upon the first day of the week, Sunday. It is true that the Jewish day is always counted from sundown to sundown, therefore meaning that the first day of the week began at sunset, Saturday evening. But the verses quoted above make it very clear what part of the day is meant. Matthew says, *"as it began to dawn."* Luke says, *"very early in the morning."* John says, *"when it was yet dark,"* seeming to infer that the dawn was near at hand. And Mark says, *"very early in the morning,"* and, *"at the rising of the sun."*

Psalm 18, which some believe to contain references to the death and resurrection of the Lord, seems to indicate that the resurrection was from the midst of great darkness, or night **(verses 9 & 11),** and that it was at the time of a great earthquake **(verse 7),** and the visitation of a heavenly being **(verses 9-10).** In verse 14 we read: *"Yea, he sent out his arrows, and scattered them; and he shot out lightnings, and discomfited them."*

Matthew 28, verses **2, 3,** and **4** read, *"And, behold, there was a great earthquake: for the angel of the Lord descended from heaven, and came and rolled back the storm from the door, and sat upon it. his countenance was like lightning, and his raiment white as snow: and for fear of him the keepers did shake, and became as dead men."*

Luke, relating the events that occurred upon the first day of the week **(Luke 24:1),** states that *"two of them went that day to a village called Emmaus."* Jesus joined them, unrecognized, and journeyed with them on their way. They visited as they walked, and, during the course of discussing the crucifixion of Jesus of Nazareth, one of the men stated, *"Beside all this, today is the third day since these things were done."* If Christ truly arose on the third day, as Paul tells us in **I Corinthians 15:4,** regardless of the exact hour that he came forth in victory from the grave, it is certain that it was not just before the sun set on Saturday. It had to have been some time after the sun had disappeared below the horizon, which brings us to Sunday.

Mark 16:9 seems to make it explicit. *"Now when Jesus was risen early the first day of the week."*

It seems that the resurrection of the Savior, the arrival of the angel, and the severe fright which befell the guards at the tomb all happened at the same time—an hour of great darkness. After Jesus had left the tomb, the guards probably revived, and, seeing that the tomb was empty, left in fear to report the event to the temple priests. These things seem to imply that tradition is probably correct in believing that Christ arose from the tomb early Sunday morning, a short while before sunrise. Then upon which day of the week was Christ actually crucified? All evidence seems to point to Thursday.

From Thursday afternoon to early Sunday morning, there are three daytime periods and three nighttime periods **(Chart 4c).** Also, the note in my Bible states that the literal translation of **Matthew 28:1** is the *"end of the sabbaths,"* or, *"The sabbaths end, the first day comes."* The plural form of the word infers that the Week of the Cross was a week that witnessed two Sabbath days. Also, if Wednesday had been the day of the Cross, and Thursday had been the special Sabbath, there is no reason why the women could not have come to the tomb, with their ointments, on Friday, between the two Sabbaths. The fact that they waited until Sunday lends weight to the supposition that the two Sabbaths were back to back.

The words of one of the two men Christ joined on the road to Emmaus seem to shine more light on the correct day of the Cross.

*"Beside all this, today is the **third day since** these things were done"* **(Luke 24:21).**

It is clear from the Bible account that Christ joined the two disciples on Sunday. If that was the third day since the day of the crucifixion, it is only logical to assume that the speaker was counting from Thursday.

Sunday was the first day from Saturday.

Sunday was the second day from Friday.

Sunday was the **third day from Thursday!**

A chronological listing of the events transpiring during the last week also promotes Thursday as the correct day of the Cross. When Friday is maintained as the crucifixion day, it is found that there is no account given for one of the days between Palm Sunday and Friday. Those who maintain that Wednesday was the day of the Cross are faced with the problem of too many days. The following paragraphs offer a listing in order of the events leading up to the resurrection.

CHRONOLOGY OF THE CRUCIFIXION WEEK

[Dates given in this study are for A.D. 30. John 12:12-50 covers from the entry into Jerusalem to the beginning of the Last Supper, not separating individual days or particular events. Events covering the trial before Pilate (2 times) and Herod are not clearly separated in all four Gospels. Therefore, all events transpiring on Thursday before the second appearance before Pilate should be studied together.]

SUNDAY, APRIL 2. The entry into Jerusalem marked a special point in the earthly ministry of Jesus when he officially offered himself to the Jewish nation as their Messiah **(Matthew 21:1-11; Mark 11:1-10; Luke 19:28-44).** Though many escorted him into the city with great acclamation, most of the crowd, urged on by the powers of the temple, soon rejected him later in the week. After entering the city, Christ went to the temple, looked around, then went to the village of Bethany **(Mark 11:12-14).**

MONDAY, APRIL 3. In the morning, as Christ journeyed toward Jerusalem, he cursed the fig tree **(Mark 11:12-14).** When he entered the temple, he drove out those marketing in money **(Matthew 21:12-13; Luke 19:45-46; Mark 11:15-17).** While there, he taught the people and healed the blind and the lame **(Luke 19:47; Matthew 21:14).** The chief priests and scribes counseled against him **(Matthew 21:15-16; Mark 11:18; Luke 19:47b-48).** He went back to Bethany that evening **(Matthew 21:17; Mark 11:19).**

TUESDAY, APRIL 4. The withered fig tree is discovered **(Matthew 21:18-22; Mark 11:20-26).** Christ returned to the temple.

He was asked about his authority **(Matthew 21:23-27; Mark 11:27-33; Luke 20:1-8)**. He taught: the parable of the two sons who worked **(Matthew 21: 28-32)**; the parable of the vineyard **(Matthew 21:33-41; Mark 12:1-9; Luke 20:9-16)**; and, the rejected stone which later became the head of the corner **(Matthew 21:42-44; Mark 12:42-44; Luke 20:10-11); Luke 20:17-18)**. The priests and the Pharisees wanted to take him, but feared the people **(Matthew 21:45-46; Mark 12:10-11; Luke 20:19)**. He taught the parable of the marriage feast **(Matthew 22:1-14)**. The Pharisees then sought to tangle him in speech and discredit him publicly: tribute to Caesar **(Matthew 22:15-22; Mark 12:13-17; Luke 20:20-26)**, and the Sadducees asked him about the woman who had many husbands **(Matthew 22:23-33; Mark 12:18-27; Luke 20:27-38)**. The lawyer (scribe) and the greatest commandment **(Matthew 22:41-46; Mark 12:35-37; Luke 20:39-44)**. Jesus upbraided the Scribes and the Pharisees **(Matthew 23:1-36; Luke 20:45-47; Mark 12:38-40)**, and complimented the widow's mite **(Mark 12:41-44; Luke 21:1-4)**. Christ lamented for Jerusalem **(Matthew 23:37-39)**. Leaving the temple, he spoke with his disciples of the great stones used in its construction **(Matthew 24:1-2; Mark 13:1-2; Luke 21:5-6)**. He privately discusses his second coming **(Matthew 24:3-51 to 25:1-46; Mark 13:3-37; Luke 21:7-36)**. Miscellaneous things and the plan to take Jesus captive **(Matthew 26:1-5; Mark 14:1-2; Luke 21:37-38 to 22:1-2)**. Back in Bethany, Mary anoints Jesus for his death **(Matthew 26:6-13; Mark 14:3-9)**. Judas talks to the priests about betraying the Lord **(Matthew 26:14-16; Mark 14:10-11; Luke 22:3-6)**.

WEDNESDAY, APRIL 5. Preparations for the Passover supper, which, in the case of the Lord and his apostles, was observed a full day early. I believe this was allowed as a special provision for those who, for some reason, could not keep the feast on its regular day. Many Jews lived in foreign countries, and travel connections were not as convenient as they usually are in our day **(Matthew 26:17-19; Mark 14:12-16; Luke 22:7-13)**. The Last Supper was observed son Wednesday evening **(Matthew 26:20-35; Mark 14:17-25; Luke 22:14-38; John 13:1 to 17:26) [John's gospel does not cover the events listed before this point]**. Jesus prayed in the garden **(Matthew

26:36-46; Mark 14:26-42; Luke 22:39-46; John 18:1). Jesus was betrayed and taken prisoner (**Matthew 26:47-56; Mark 14:43-52; Luke 22:47-53; John 18:2-12**). He was taken before the Sanhedrin, and Peter soon denied him. The trial continued through the night (**Matthew 26:57-75; Mark 14:53-72; Luke 22:54-71; John 18: 13-27**).

THURSDAY, APRIL 6. When morning came, Christ was led before Pilate (**Matthew 27:1-2; Mark 15:1-14; Luke 23:1-6**). Judas regretted his deed and hanged himself (**Matthew 27:3-10**). Jesus was sent to Herod, but then returned to Pilate (**Luke 23:7-12**). Jesus was examined before Pilate (**Matthew 27:11-26; Luke 23:13-25; John 18:28 through 19:16**). Christ was scourged (**Matthew 27:27-30; Mark 15:15-19**). Jesus carries his cross to Calvary (**Matthew 27:31-32; Mark 15:20-23; Luke 23:26-32; John 19:17**). He is crucified (**Matthew 27:33-50; Mark 15:24-37; Luke 23:33-46, except verse 45; John 19:18-30**). The Temple veil is rent (**Matthew 27:51; Mark 15:38; Luke 23:45**). The Roman soldier proclaimed him the Son of God (**Matthew 27:54; Mark 15:39; Luke 23:47**). The legs of the thieves were broken and the side of Christ was pierced (**John 19:31-37**). The Burial (**Matthew 27:55-61; Mark 15:40-47; Luke 23:48-56; John 19:38-42**).

FRIDAY, APRIL 7. The tomb was sealed (**Matthew 27:62-66**).

SATURDAY, APRIL 8. No events are given for this day.

SUNDAY, APRIL 9. Christ arose from the grave!!! (**Matthew 28:1-20; Mark 16:1-20; Luke 24:1-53; John 24:1 to 21:25**). Many graves were also opened immediately after the Resurrection of Christ, these people being seen by many (**Matthew 27:52-53**).

The crucifixion occurred during the week of the Passover feast. Therefore, it is not difficult to affix proper Jewish calendar dates to the days, for the Jewish feast days were observed according to a very rigorous schedule. The schedule is given in **Exodus 12:1-14,** and in **Leviticus 23:4-11.** The Passover Lamb was set aside upon the tenth day of the month (Nisan). It was slain upon the fourteenth day of the month. If these values are applied to the week of the Cross, it is found that they align as shown in **Chart 5.** Sunday, April 2, was also the tenth day of Nisan; and Thursday, April 6, was also the fourteenth day of Nisan. On the tenth day of the Jewish month, Christ rode into the city of Jerusalem, presenting himself to the Jewish nation. From this point in his life, there could be no turning back or further delay in the destiny of the Cross. The stage was set for his crucifixion, and it would now come to pass upon schedule, as surely as the Passover Lamb was destined for the slaughter. Even as Passover lambs were being put to death on the Day of Preparation, the fourteenth day of Nisan, Christ, God's sacrificial lamb, died exactly as prescribed by Mosaic Law.

It is interesting to note that the Feast of Passover was to be observed upon a precise day of the month (Nisan 14). Also, the Feast of Unleavened Bread was to begin on a precise day (Nisan 15). But the ceremony of the Waving of the Sheaf was to be upon the **"morrow after the Sabbath."** It was not designated by an exact date! This was the Feast of First Fruits, and was a shadow of the resurrection of Christ **(Leviticus 23:10-11; I Corinthians 15:23).** It is evident that the foreknowledge of God looked forward to the time of the Cross, and prepared the words of Leviticus to allow for a week with two Sabbaths followed by the resurrection on Sunday, "the morrow after the Sabbath."

Chart 5
THE WEEK OF THE CROSS
(30 A.D.)

	*_SUN_*	*_MON_*	*_TUE_*	*_WED_*	*_THU_*	*_FRI_*	*_SAT_*	*_SUN_*
April	2	3	4	5	6	7	8	9
Nisan	10	11	12	13	14	15	16	17

The 8 days of "Passion Week" began with Palm Sunday and ended with Resurrection Sunday. Dates according to the modern system are given parallel to dates of the Jewish Calendar for the year of the Cross. Jesus was crucified on April 6, and arose from the grave on **April 9.**

Further evidence of a Thursday crucifixion comes from science itself. In 1974, a report was published in newspapers telling of a special scientific study researching the time of the Cross. The conclusion was that Jesus was crucified on the fifth day of the week, Thursday, April 6, A.D. 30. The reasons for this conclusion were based primarily upon modern knowledge of the movements of the moon, employing modern computer-calculated tables of new and full moons from B.C. 1001, to A.D. 1651.

The Passover was determined from the time of the first new moon after the spring equinox. Therefore, it is now possible to determine the exact day used by the Jews to celebrate the holy feast. The article is reproduced in the following paragraphs as printed in the April 13, 1974 edition of the "Lawton Morning Press."

CRUCIFIXION ON THURSDAY, SCIENTIST CLAIMS
By George W. Cornell

New York (AP)—A scientist, using new tables of dating figured on a computer, has concluded that the crucifixion of Jesus occurred on the fifth day of the week, a Thursday, April 6, 30 A.D., and not on Friday as commonly assumed, "Up to now, we didn't have the hard facts to fasten to, but now we have them," says Roger Rusk, a Knoxville, Tenn., physicist.

His deductions also would mean that Jesus lay in the tomb a full three days as he had foreseen—instead of the 36 hours supposed in church tradition. By it, churches observe this Friday to mark the day he died.

"But the movements of the moon don't provide the occasion for it then," Rusk said in a telephone interview. "Putting together what we now know, it's evident the day was Thursday." He also concludes that the year—not previously fixed precisely—was 30 A.D.

In making his assessments, he used newly calculated tables of new and full moons from 1001 B.C. to A.D. 1651, as determined on a sophisticated computer by Herman H. Goldstein at the Institute of Advanced Studies, Princeton, N.J.

"It had never been done before," Rusk said, adding that the new tables provide the first exact sequence of new moons by which dates were set in ancient Judaism in the time of Jesus.

"They kept a lunar calendar and went entirely by the moon," he said. Since Jesus died on an afternoon before the sunset beginning of Passover, just what day it was hinges on when Passover started that year and that in turn, depends on the time of the new moon—the added key applied by Rusk.

Rusk, emeritus professor of physics at the University of Tennessee where he taught for 28 years, details his findings in a recent issue of the evangelical weekly, Christianity Today, published in Washington, D.C.

Although various Gospel references indicate the general period in which Jesus died, Rusk says the lunar data pins the plausible time down to the year 30 A.D., as well as pointing to Thursday, and that maintenance of the Friday tradition has made it necessary to assume an inactive "day of silence" in Jesus' days in Jerusalem before his arrest.

However, the Gospel never mentions such a day, Rusk notes, adding that "it is an invention designed to support" the traditional thesis of a Friday crucifixion.

That thesis "also depends on another dodge," he said, citing the traditional assumption that from Friday mid-afternoon until Sunday morning constitute three days that Jesus was in the tomb before his resurrection.

Actually, that time interval is one full day and fractions of two others.

"It just won't do," Rusk said. "But church people have lived with it and rationalized it to justify their Friday services."

Rusk, a Presbyterian, said he isn't proposing ant changes in the schedule of church observances. "It would be nice, but I'm not urging it," he said. "What happened is more important than when it's celebrated."

In his deductions, he notes that Passover begins on the 14th day of the Jewish month of Nisan, whose start is determined by the spring new moon. The new tables show Nisan 14th came on Thursday only in the year 30 A.D. in the general span of years when the crucifixion could have occurred.

In that general time bracket, Nisan 14th occurs on Friday in 26 A.D., but "this is regarded as too early," and also in 33 A.D., but this is too late." Thus the moon data pointed to Thursday, he says, and in turn to 30 A.D.

[END OF REPRODUCED ARTICLE]

Jesus made his triumphal entry into Jerusalem, riding upon an ass, on April 2, A.D. 30. He went to the temple, spent some time there, then departed to Bethany where he spent the night.

On Monday, April 3, in route to Jerusalem in the morning, he passed a certain fig tree, and cursed it for bearing no fruit. Going on into the city, he entered the temple. He drove out those carrying on practices unsuitable for that holy place. He remained in the temple area, teaching and healing the blind and lame who came to him. It is at this point we are told that the chief priests and scribes counseled privately against him. He returned to Bethany for the night.

On Tuesday, April 4, as Christ and those with him walked from Bethany to Jerusalem, the disciples noticed the fig tree withered, and marveled at it. On this day, Christ spent a great deal of time in the temple, and many of his teachings are recorded from this visit.

He told the parables of the two sons, the vineyard, and the marriage feast. He spoke of his authority, the stone which became the head of the corner, paying tribute to Caesar, the resurrection and marriage, the Great Commandment, and asked them whose son Christ was. He upbraided the scribes and Pharisees, admonished the Widow's mite, and lamented for the city of Jerusalem.

The priests and Pharisees would have taken him prisoner, but they feared the multitude of people who praised him.

He retired to the Mount of Olives where he taught his disciples many of the great prophecies concerning his Second Coming. That evening, in Bethany, Judas was offended when Jesus rebuked him for criticizing the woman who had anointed his head with ointment. Judas then went to lay plans for the betrayal.

On Wednesday, April 5, special preparations were made for the Passover supper. That evening, in the upper room and after the ceremonial meal was finished, Jesus then instructed the apostles concerning the Lord's Supper. Judas left to do his deed, and Christ led the disciples to the Garden of Gethsemane, where he prayed.

While he was here, apart from the supposed protection of the multitudes, a large number of people came (the number almost certainly comprised of the temple guard and Jewish allies to the higher temple hierarchy), bearing swords and staffs, and took him prisoner by order of the chief priests and elders of the people. He was led before the Sanhedrin, where, sometime that night, he was declared a blasphemer and worthy of death. When morning came, the Jewish officials took him to Pilate, the representative of Rome, for under Roman law the Jews were not allowed to condemn a man to death. But Pilate, recognizing a potential matter he did not desire to become involved in, sent him to Herod. Herod, disappointed because Christ would not perform a miracle for his entertainment, sent him back to Pilate. Finally, yielding to the demands of the crowd, Pilate delivered Jesus to the will of the mob, and Christ was nailed to the Cross of Calvary at 9:00 A.M., Thursday, April 6, A.D. 30. He died at 3:00 P.M., after hanging upon the Cross for six hours.

April 6, A.D. 30, was the 96th day of the year, and, the exact numerical figure for the time of his death may be written, A.D. 29.2619863. This may be regarded as the moment in the history of the world that the ponderous debt of sin was eternally marked **PAID IN FULL!**

James F. Webb

Chapter 7
Are there Signs of His Return?

"Watch therefore, for ye know neither the day nor the hour wherein the Son of Man cometh" **(Matthew 25:13.)**

There have been many who have attempted to foretell the exact time of the Lord's return to the earth, going to great lengths and efforts to fully understand the Bible's words about the Rapture and the appearance of Christ at the close of the Tribulation. I was once caught up in the quest, myself, but came to realize that God does not desire that certain things be revealed before they actually happen. Most of all, I believe this is true concerning the Rapture.

However, the Revelation of Christ at the close of the seven-year Tribulation Period is another matter. Though I cannot say that the exact day of his coming is now known, I can say, with some confidence, that a time will come when men will know at least the approximate date of his return to the Mount of Olives. Daniel the Prophet, over five centuries before Christ, wrote of it in the twelfth chapter of Daniel.

"Then I Daniel looked, and, behold, there stood other two, the one on this side of the bank of the river, and the other on that side of the river. And one said to the man clothed in linen, which was upon the waters of the river, How long shall it be to the end of these wonders? And I heard the man clothed in linen, which was upon the waters of the river, when he held up his right hand and his left hand unto heaven, and sware by him that liveth for ever that it shall be for a time, times, and an half; and when he shall have accomplished to scatter the power of the holy people, all these things shall be finished. And I heard, but I understood not: then said I, O my Lord, what shall be the end of these things? And he said, Go thy way, Daniel: for the words are closed up and sealed till the time of the end. Many shall be purified, and made white, and tried; but the wicked shall do wickedly; and none of the wicker shall understand; but the wise shall under-stand. And from the time that the daily sacrifice shall be taken away,

and the abomination that maketh desolate set up, there shall be a thousand two hundred and ninety days. Blessed is he that waiteth, and cometh to the thousand three hundred and five and thirty days" **(Daniel 12:5-12).**

In reality, these verses give us three intervals of time, which are: 1,260 days (the time, times, and a half); 1,290 days; and 1,335 days. Each interval seems to be counted from the same moment in history— the day when the Antichrist declares himself to be a god, and sets up his image in the holy place. It is the Abomination of Desolation, spoken of by both Daniel and Jesus.

"And [the False Prophet] *deceiveth them that dwell on the earth by the means of those miracles which he had power to do in the sight of the beast; saying to them that dwell on the earth, that they should make an image to the beast, which had the wound by a sword, and did live. And he had power to give life unto the image of the beast, that the image of the beast should both speak, and cause that as many as would not worship the image of the beast should be killed" (***Revelation 13:14-15).**

It is apparent that Christ will return to earth at the close of these intervals, but choosing the correct span of time has divided some in their thinking. Most Bible theologians are in mystery concerning the 1,335-day interval, but agree that it is a very blessed moment, with the harsh events and fearful tensions of the Tribulation and the Battle of Armageddon already in the past. The same theologians are in mild opposition concerning the other two intervals.

Some believe the events described in Revelation should always be taken in the exact order they are presented in. Others think that, in certain cases, a particular subject is followed through until that topic has been exhausted, much as history books often follow the policy of pursuing a particular subject through to its end without regard to other events unfolding at the same time. In the study of the Book of Revelation, I fine that I am inclined to lean somewhat toward the thought that some things in the last book of the Bible are presented with an over-all view rather than exact chronological order.

For example:

"And I beheld when he had opened the sixth seal, and lo, there was a great earthquake; and the sun became black as sackcloth of hair, and the moon became as blood; And the stars of heaven fell unto the earth, even as a fig tree casteth her untimely figs, when she is shaken of a mighty wind. And the heaven departed as a scroll when it is rolled together; and every mountain and island were moved out of their places. And the kings of the earth, and the great men, and the rich men, and the chief captains, and the mighty men. Hid themselves in the dens and in the rocks of the mountains; And said to the mountains and rocks, Fall on us, and hide us from the face of him that sitteth on the throne, and from the wrath of the Lamb. For the great day of his wrath is come; and who shall be able to stand?" **(Revelation 6:12-17)**.

"Immediately after the tribulation of those days shall the sun be darkened, and the moon shall not give her light, and the stars of heaven, and the powers of the heavens shall be shaken: And then shall appear the sigh of the Son of man in heaven: and then shall all the tribes of earth mourn, and they shall see the Son of man coming in the clouds of heaven with power and great glory" **(Matthew 24:29-30)**.

"And I saw heaven opened, and behold a white horse; and he that sat upon him was called Faithful and True, and in righteousness he doth judge and make war. His eyes were as a flame of fire, and on his head were many crowns; and he had a name written, that no man knew, but he himself. And he was clothed with a vesture dipped in blood: and his name is called the Word of God. And the armies which were in heaven followed him upon white horses, clothed in fine linen, white and clean. And out of his mouth goeth a sharp sword, that with it he should smite the nations; and he shall rule them with a rod of iron: and he treadeth the winepress of the fierceness and wrath of Almighty God. And he hath on his vesture and on his thigh a name written, KING OF KINGS, AND LORD OF LORDS" **(Revelation 19:11-16)**.

I believe these three different quotes from the Bible speak of the same thing; the Coming of Christ at the close of the period of tribulation (the words of Jesus in **Matthew**); the verses from the sixth chapter of Revelation; and, the verses showing Christ and the armies of heaven coming to earth in the nineteenth chapter of Revelation. So, it would seem logical that most of the things written in Revelation, between the verses of the sixth chapter, and the nineteenth chapter.

Which brings us back to the three intervals of time. Some Bible scholars believe that Christ will return to the earth at the close of the 1,260 days following the Antichrist's blasphemous act of Abomination. Others think he will come after 1,290 days. Though I am not dogmatic about it, I do believe the longer of these two intervals is the correct one, but only because I place the ministry of the "two witnesses," spoken of in **Zechariah 4 and Revelation 11,** to begin at the time of the Abomination, also.

The army of the Antichrist will overrun Jerusalem, and, as shown in **Revelation 11:2**, he will hold it for 1,260 days (the Second Times of the Gentiles), counting from the time he defiles the "Holy Place," and claims that he is God and the true messiah of Israel. But he will not be without opposition. **Revelation 11** speaks of two witnesses who stand up against him.

"And I will give power unto my two witnesses, and they shall prophecy a thousand two hundred and threescore days, clothed in sackcloth. These are the two olive trees **[Zechariah 4]**, *and the two candlesticks standing before the God of the earth. And if any man will hurt them, fire proceedeth out of their mouth, and devoureth their enemies: and if any man will hurt them, he must in this manner be killed. These have power to shut heaven, that it rain not in the days of their prophecy; and have power over waters to turn them to blood, and to spit the earth with all plagues, as often as they will. And when they shall have finished their testimony, the beast that ascendeth out of the bottomless pit shall make war against them, and shall overcome them, and kill them. And their dead bodies shall lie in the street of the great city, which spiritually is called Sodom and Egypt, where also our Lord was crucified. And they of the people and kindreds and tongues and nations shall see their dead bodies three days and a half, and shall not suffer their dead bodies to be put in graves. And they that dwell upon the earth shall rejoice over them, and make merry, and shall send gifts one to another* [we are reminded of the renewed friendship of Pilate

and Herod after the trial of Christ]; *because these two prophets tormented them that dwelt on the earth on the earth. And after three days and a half the spirit of life from God entered into them, and they stood upon their feet; and great fear fell upon them which saw them. And they heard a great voice from heaven saying unto them, Come up hither. And they ascended up into heaven in a cloud; and their enemies beheld them. And the same hour was there a great earthquake, and the tenth part of the city fell, and in the earthquake were slain of men seven thousand: and the remnant were affrighted, and gave glory to the God of heaven"* **(Revelation 11:3-13).**

If the ministry of the "two witnesses" does begin immediately following the Abomination of Desolation, as I believe it does, it is difficult to accept that Christ will return to the earth at the close of the 1,260 days. This is simply because the witnesses are slain at the end of this period of time, then, their dead bodies are allowed to lie in the street of Jerusalem for another three and a half days. During this time, their enemies rejoice greatly. It is not possible that Jesus Christ has already returned to the earth, for there will be no rejoicing of the forces of Satan in the Lord's presence. In the verses already quoted earlier in this chapter, from Revelation 6 and Matthew 24, we see that great fear and dread fall upon the enemies of the Lord when they see his true power and behold him coming in the clouds of Heaven. If he comes after the resurrection of the two witnesses, then he will come at a later point than the 1,260 days.

In **Revelation 11:13,** we are told of a great earthquake which destroys a tenth of the city of Jerusalem and kills 7,000 men. We are told that those who survive were filled with fear, and gave glory to the God of Heaven! This is at last the terms of the words spoken by Jesus as he stood overlooking the city in the days just before his Crucifixion.

"Behold, your house is left unto you desolate. For I say unto you, Ye shall not see me henceforth, till ye shall say, blessed is he that cometh in the name of the Lord." **(Matthew 23:38-39).**

These are the same words proclaimed by the crowd as Jesus rode into Jerusalem a few days before his crucifixion. Then, the proclamation was shouted by individual persons, but, at the close of the Tribulation Period, it will be declared by the nation of Israel. They will finally confess that Jesus is the true Messiah, and they will give glory to the God of Heaven! This is the event the Lord has waited for! The glorious happening of the ages! When Jesus Christ will return to the earth to establish his kingdom!

When Israel turns to Jesus Christ, the true Messiah, the doors of heaven will open and the Lord will be seen riding upon a great white horse, approaching the earth at the head of the armies of heaven. I do not know how much time will elapse between the first sighting of the Lord's coming and the moment he actually touches down on the Mount of Olives, but I suspect it will not be long. I do not believe it will be in "the twinkling of an eye," as it will be at the time of the Rapture, for, as earth rotates on its polar axis, I think he will allow the whole earth to see his actual presence in the sky. Many evil men who have opposed the preaching of his name will, at that time, tremble in fear and seek to hide themselves in any way they hope is possible.

The greatest armies of earth shall have already gathered in the expansive valley of Megiddo to the north. The remaining forces of the Antichrist will be there along with the armies of the "kings of the east." Their original reason for gathering in that area shall have been to wage war with one another, to settle the matter of world supremacy. But now, a new problem has arisen in the unexpected return of Jesus Christ to the earth, and their common hatred of the Heavenly King seems to unite them in an unholy bond. The Battle of Armageddon soon follows, and we have already studied the result of that conflict in other pages.

So, if we adopt the theory that Christ will return to the earth after the interval of 1,290 days, those who mark the day of the Abomination of Desolation may also assume that the Lord's return will be at the close of that number of days.

There will be an even shorter time period evident to those who dwell in and around Jerusalem in those days, for they will witness the slaying of the two witnesses after 1,260 days, and will be able to count the remaining 30 days to the Second Coming from that event. Their hearts and souls will surely be filled with great joy and relief when they see the Savior actually appear in the sky, but, the Tribulation will be such a frightful period of death and destruction to live through that it would be far better to accept the Lord as Savior before the Rapture of the Church, and then return to the earth as part of that great army of heaven.

But these intervals of time, though known to the Church, are still a complete mystery to us who live before the Rapture, for we are unable to relate them to an actual date from which to count. The intervals of time are given mainly to the Jews, and not to the Church.

But are there other "Signs of the Times" which can be studied by the Church, by which we can "know" that the Rapture is not very distant in the future? The answer, of course, is yes! There are very many of them, some quite general in nature while others are so specific that they leave little doubt in the observer's mind, if the observer will view them with open eyes and unprejudiced heart. A list of general signs pertaining primarily to personal traits follows.

1. Men shall be "Lovers of their Own Selves" **(II Timothy 3:2)**.
2. Men shall be "Covetous" **(II Timothy 3:2)**.
3. Men shall be "Boasters" **(II Timothy 3:2)**.
4. Men shall be "Proud" **(II Timothy 3:2)**.
5. Men shall be "Blasphemers" **(II Timothy 3:2)**.
6. Men shall be "Disobedient to Parents" **(II Timothy 3:2)**.
7. Men shall be "Unthankful" **(II Timothy 3:2)**.
8. Men shall be "Unholy" **(II Timothy 3:2)**.
9. Men shall be "Without Natural Affection" **(II Timothy 3:3)**.
10. Men shall be "Trucebreakers" **(II Timothy 3:3)**.
11. Men shall be "False Accusers" **(II Timothy 3:3)**.
12. Men shall be "Incontinent" **(II Timothy 3:3)**.
13. Men shall be "Fierce" **(II Timothy 3:3)**.
14. Men shall be "Despisers of Those That Are Good" **(II Timothy 3:3)**.
15. Men shall be "Traitors" **(II Timothy 3:4)**.
16. Men shall be "Heady" **(II Timothy 3:4)**.
17. Men shall be "Highminded" **(II Timothy 3:4)**.

18. Men shall be "Lovers of Pleasure More than Lovers of God" **(II Timothy 3-4)**.
19. Men shall have a "Form of Godliness," but "Shall Deny the Power Thereof" **(II Timothy 3:5)**.
20. There shall be "False Teachers" **(II Peter 2:1-2)**.

It seems logical that this particular prediction applies to at least two classes of teacher: (one) the religious teacher (or person) who has drifted away from what the Bible actually tells us, and, (two) the secular teacher (or person) who is carried away by the "false" side of science, and instructs his or her pupils against theories of creation, favoring modern theories of evolution.

It is of course apparent that all of the twenty items listed above have probably been in the world from the very earliest times of history. They will also be in the world in the "latter" days, or the time just before the Lord returns to the earth. So, one might argue how can these be prophecies which prepare us for the soon return of Jesus?

They, in themselves, do not tell us by themselves that we are in the last days. They merely describe what the social climate of those days will be like, and, even though these traits have blemished the character of man throughout history, they are to be especially predominant in the days before the Rapture.

The author of this work is not a young man, but neither do I consider myself as completely "over-the hill." I was born into the world during the 1930's. President Roosevelt was in the White House in Washington, and things were beginning to climb out of the great depression which had deflated the economy for a few years. My father worked hard as a section hand for the Frisco Railroad, so I do not remember ever going hungry. We ate a lot of beans and cornbread (which remain to this day one of my favorite meals) but we got by. However, even then, I am certain the list given above found many living examples in the civilization in which I grew up. But, I have honestly noticed a tremendous difference in that by-gone age and the age of today. I am equally certain that any reader who has attained an age which is at least near adulthood, or slightly beyond, if he will strive to be completely truthful with himself, will have to admit that the presented "list" is more descriptive of the present age in which we now live than the age of the past few generations preceding the present. While there are certainly many fine examples of humanity yet present in the world, the overall estimate of man's nature seems to have slipped toward the "Twenty List."

James F. Webb

Chapter 8
More Specific Examples of the Signs of the Times

The preceding chapter presented a list of twenty signs which may be considered fairly common to most of the ages of mankind. While it is true that those signs and conditions have existed throughout most of recorded history, it is equally true that never before have all existed so conspicuously and in such magnitude as in the present age. But there are other signs given us in the Bible which are more specific than those listed in the chapter before this one. Some of the more conspicuous ones are presented in the following pages.

21. There shall be Scoffers concerning the Second Coming of the Lord **(II Peter 3:3-4)**. Those who follow false teachers find themselves in a world where God does not exist, or, at least they do not believe God exists. Therefore, the "scoffer" does not believe Christ will ever return to the earth. He believes all things will simply continue as they are now. It is a sad thing to recognize the truth that there are even Christians who do not accept the thought that Jesus will physically return to the earth and establish the Millennial Kingdom. They believe that we, at death, leave the world and go into a heavenly location, there to be in the presence of God. However, the Bible clearly states that Christ will return to the earth to set up his kingdom.
22. There shall be an increase in Spiritualism **(I Timothy 4:1)**. This actually relates to the "Days of Noah" which will be studied later, but it is apparent to anyone who keeps his eyes open that many people of the present age, turning away from the true God of heaven, seek to fill the gap created within them with false ideas of spiritualism, astrology, fortune telling, and devil worship.
23. The Laodicean Church shall be prominent **(Revelation 3:14-22)**. The letters to the seven churches seem to describe seven spiritual conditions found in individual

churches. It is also believed that the seven churches reveal to us seven steps in the history between the First-Century Church and the Church of the Last Days. Though all of these traits have existed in churches through time, the Laodicean Church seems to point to the overall condition of most of the churches in our age (lukewarm, proud in their riches, thinking they have need of nothing, and not realizing they have forsaken a close relationship with the Lord and do not see they are actually wretched, miserable, poor, blind, and naked).

24. The following "signs of the times" need very little or no explanation:
25. Great fortunes will be amassed using fraud (**James 5:1-6**).
26. There shall be famines (**Matthew 24:7**).
27. There shall be pestilences (**Matthew 24:7**).
28. There shall be earthquakes (**Matthew 24:7**).
29. There shall be trouble among the nations of earth (**Matthew 24:7**).
30. There shall be wars and rumors of wars (**Matthew 24:6**).
31. There shall be False Prophets (**Matthew 24:11**).
32. There shall be many False Christs (**Matthew 24:5**). We have already witnessed several cult leaders who have lead many to their destruction deceiving them into believing that they were the Messiah, or Jesus Christ.
33. There shall be Automobiles (**Nahum 2:3-4**).
34. There is a possible reference to Airplanes in the leaping chariots of **Nahum 3:2.**
35. An early prediction by God of the telephone, radio, and other modern conveniences (**Job 38:35**). Although no reference is made in this verse to the last days, it does seem to fit well into the present time.
36. People shall run to and fro (**Daniel 12:4**).
37. Knowledge shall be increased (**Daniel 12:4 & II Timothy 3:7**).

38. There shall be great Apostasy due to two main reasons. Sin and a lack of love for God **(Matthew 24:12 & II Thessalonians 2:3).**
39. Probably, the Church will not witness most of the following signs come into fulfillment, for they fall more after the Rapture than before. But we can already see the world striving to move toward several of them.
40. Perilous Times shall come in the last days **(II Timothy 3:1).**
41. There shall be Persecution and Betrayal **(Matthew 24:9-10).**
42. There shall be Fearful Sights and Great Signs **(Luke 21:11 & 25).** This prophecy not only includes signs 25, 26, and 27, given above, but includes signs in the sun, the moon, and the stars, distress of nations, perplexity, with the sea and the waves roaring.
43. Men's hearts failing them for fear **(Luke 21:26 & Isaiah 24:17-18).**
44. The following are special and very specific types of signs, some unfolding, or beginning to unfold before the Rapture of the Church, while others take place during the Tribulation Period.
45. The Revival of the Hebrew language **(Zephaniah 3:9).** The native language of the Jewish people has continued to exist during the centuries following the destruction wrought upon their nation by the Romans in A.D. 70. However, it had greatly diminished in use by the twentieth century, Jewish people primarily using the speech of the nations they had been absorbed into. As Jewish people have returned to the land of their heritage in vast numbers, and that land has been restored to Israel, the Jewish language, after the slow elapse of almost nineteen centuries, has once more become a national language.
46. 43. The days before the Coming of the Lord shall be as it was in the Days of Noah before the Flood **(Matthew 24:37-39).** We are given a brief account of Cain's

descendants in **Genesis 4.** By these few words, we can understand that the period of time before the Flood was a time of a civilization advancing in skills at a very rapid rate. Population had advanced to such numbers that people began to dwell in cities as well as in the country. Men made advancement in fine arts as well as in the technical skills. Jubal was said to be the father of *"all such as handle the harp and organ."* Jubal was a cattleman, undoubtedly using that talent to build a business selling portions of his herds to others as a source of food. There were advances in the use of metals, for Tubal-cain was an instructor in manufacturing articles of brass and iron.

In **Genesis 6,** we are given an account concerning certain *"mysterious"* marriages which occurred between the *"Sons of God"* and the *"daughters of men."* Some Bible students believe that these marriages were instigated between sons of the line of Cain and daughters from the line of Seth. There is no reason to suppose that such marriages between the descendants of the two sons of Adam did not occur, as well as marriages between the lines of all the other unnamed sons of Adam and Eve **(Genesis 5:4** tells us that, after the birth of Seth, Adam lived eight-hundred years and fathered more sons and daughters. In fact, I believe Jewish tradition has taught that Adam had forty children in all). But these marriages would not have created problems more than we witness today when marriages take place between people who are faithful to God, and people who have strayed away from God. The words in **Genesis 6:4** seem to imply that there was more to these marriages than some believe.

"There were giants in the earth in those days, and also after that, when the sons of God came in unto the daughters of men, and they bare children to them, the same became mighty men which were of old, men of renown." **(Genesis 6:4).**

Although there is a division among many theologians, this verse seems to suggest that these marriages were more than normal unions between mankind. In the Old Testament, the use of the term, "Sons of God," is applied almost exclusively to angels. In the book of Job, it seems evident that the words are used in this manner to describe a special gathering before God's throne in heaven, with Satan among them, for the souls of men had not yet ascended to the throne of God but were housed in the Bosom of Abraham (in an earthly location across a great gulf from hell) until after the Cross. Therefore, in this particular case, the *"Sons of God"* must have applied to angelic beings. Because of this, many theologians teach, in contrast to the theory of marriages between the seed of Cain and Seth, that the questionable unions were between certain angelic beings and the daughters of men. The consequences of such marriages apparently had the results explained to us in **Genesis 6:4** (above). It would also explain certain legends that have come down to us, adopted especially by the Greek culture to form the stories of their multiple gods and their intermingling with mankind to produce such "heroes" as Hercules and Atlas. The truly great strong man of the Bible, born of natural parents, was, of course, Samson, who was strengthened by the Spirit of God. He should not be confused with the "men of renown" who lived before the Flood.

Whether one embraces one theory or the other, it yet remains that unnatural alliances seemed to have occurred, and suggests that those marriages created an "unholy" line of people. It was considered so extreme that the only apparent way to cleanse the human race was to exterminate it with the Flood. Only Noah (and his family) were found *"just"* and *"perfect in his generations."*

There are aspects of this "sign" which will be examined to greater depth in a later chapter, but the words of Christ, taken at sight as given in the book of Matthew, show us that life will continue in a way considered "normal," even as it has throughout history. People will be continuing in their usual activities, going to work, seeking entertainment, marrying, finding pleasure in the accumulation of material things as life goes on, completely unaware of impending doom.

44. The Rebirth of Israel as a Nation. If a person truly wants to see the living proof of God's Eternal Word, all he has to do is look at the nation of Israel. The written words of Biblical prophets have long proclaimed that the nation of the Jews would one day spring into

existence once more, even though its people have been scattered throughout the countries of the world for many centuries. In **Ezekiel 37:1-3,** we read, *"The hand of the Lord was upon me, and carried me out in the spirit of the Lord, and set me down in the midst of the valley which was full of bones. And caused me to pass by them round about: and, behold, there were very many in the open valley; and, lo, they were very dry. And he said unto me, Son of man, can these bones live?"*

The prophet had been told of the restoration of the Jewish nation in **Ezekiel 36:24-38.** Now, Ezekiel is given the method in vivid symbolism. The dry bones of the valley represent the whole of the twelve tribes, buried around the world in many nations. The words of **Ezekiel 37:11-14** are quite clear and specific.

"Then he said unto me, Son of man, these bones are the whole house of Israel: behold, they say, Our bones are dried, and our hope is lost: we are cut off for our parts. Therefore prophecy and say unto them, Thus saith the Lord God: Behold, O my people, I will open your graves [the nations], *and cause you to come up out of your graves, and bring you into the land of Israel. And ye shall know that I am the Lord, when I have opened your graves, O my people, and brought you up out of your graves, And shall put my spirit in you, and ye shall live, and I shall place you in your own land: then shall ye know that I have spoken it, and performed it, saith the Lord."*

If a person desires to be aware of the approaching Second coming of the Lord Jesus Christ, he only has to watch history as it unfolds in the Middle-East. Most of the important events of the next few years, affecting the entire globe, will take place there. In fact, the world will revolve around Jerusalem for the next Millennium, for it is from that city that the blessed King of Kings will rule for one-thousand years. The Jewish race, though the powers of Satan and of men have sought to eliminate it from the face of the earth, will survive through all eternity.

45. The invasion from the North **(Ezekiel 38 & 39).** The idea that these chapters speak of an invasion by Russia into the land of Israel is not a modern-day concoction. It has been around for a very long time, even well before the land of Russia was a nation remotely to be

reckoned with as a worthy force. The invading nation is clearly marked by the names of two of the cities within that country B Meshech and Tubal (the ancient names of Moscow and Tobolsk). In its original form, the word translated in the King James Bible as "chief" is actually "Rosh," the same word the ancient Russian tribes applied to themselves. So, instead of the *"chief* prince of Meshech and Tubal," we would not be amiss if we read it as the "Russian prince of Moscow and Tobolsk."

We see the approach of that in invasion even today, in Russia's strong backing of Israel's enemies. In spite of political changes in the recently communist country, things appear to be unstable. If Russia's economy continues to falter, national policies may change. If things continue to go in favor of Israel, and if Russia, for some reason, thinks that nations friendly to Israel will not interfere, the armies of the north will surely march toward the Holy Land. When that invasion does come, the Bible tells us it will fail with a very great destruction of the aggressor's forces. Ezekiel 39:2 tells us that the defeat of the invading army will be so great that only one-sixth of that army will survive.

I do not know when that invasion will take place, except to believe that it will transpire around a certain seven year peace pact instigated with Israel, brought about by the Antichrist. I do not know if the Church will witness that invasion or not, for it is possible that the Rapture will take place before that event. I do not know if the defeat of the invading army will be brought about by God or by the military might of some worldly power. But, I do believe that the collapse of the Russian military force will aid in opening the door for the rise of Antichrist to power.

46. The Eight-Days of Man and the Tabernacle. In chapter two, mention was made concerning the "Eight-Days of Man." The title is arrived at by adding together the seven Great Days of the Great Week (the seven Great Days from the Garden of Eden during which mankind will be upon the earth), and the seventh day of the "Creation," during which Adam and Eve lived in the garden. Whether or not that particular seventh day was a thousand-year day or a twenty-four hour period of time does not disallow the theory that mankind, descended from Adam and Eve, has been upon the earth for Eight Great Days.

It has long been pointed out that the Wilderness Tabernacle had incorporated into it many things that prophesied of Christ. The very sacrifices and rituals performed in it by the priests pictured to us the sacrifice of the Son of God upon the Cross of Calvary—the sacrificial lamb who gave his life that all mankind might benefit from it. In the services of the tabernacle, men brought offerings to the priest who made sacrifices and presented them to God for the sins of individual men. But Christ, the perfect lamb, served a dual role, performing both as high priest and sacrifice in that he willingly laid down his very own body as the supreme and eternal offering for the sin of mankind.

"And every priest standeth daily ministering and offering oftentimes the same sacrifices, which can never take away sins: but this man, after he had offered one sacrifice for sins forever, sat down on the right hand of God" **(Hebrews 10:11-12).**

When God told Moses to build the tabernacle, he instructed him to use certain very precise measurements for the over-all perimeter and the rooms of the building within. The outer court, enclosed by curtains but open above, measured 100-cubits long by 50-cubits wide. Two covered, joined rooms sat in the west half of the courtyard. The sanctuary, or Holy Place, measured 20-cubits long by 10-cubits wide by 10-cubits high. The Holy of Holies, which held the Ark of the covenant, measured 10-cubits long by 10-cubits wide by 10-cubits high.

The area of the courtyard (found by multiplying the length by the width) is shown to be 5,000 square cubits. The volume of the sanctuary (20 x 10 x 10) is shown to be 2,000 cubic cubits. The volume of the Holy of Holies (10 x 10 x 10) is shown to be 1,000 cubit cubits. It would appear that the Wilderness Tabernacle does support the theory of the Eight Great Days in its measurements: the courtyard showing us the five great days from the placement of Adam and Eve in the Garden of Eden; the sanctuary showing us the two great days of the Church Age; and the Holy of holies (where one went to be in the very presence of the Lord) showing us the great day of the Millennium, when Christ, in person, dwells with us on the earth. Though we do not know exactly how God measures these great days, it is evident that his return is drawing very near.

Chapter 9
The Sign of the Times of the Gentiles, and the Seventy Years

"Jerusalem shall be trodden down of the Gentiles, until the times of the Gentiles be fulfilled" **(Luke 21:24)**.

When Solomon died in the year B.C. 975, the Hebrew nation split apart into two separate kingdoms. The northern kingdom was known as Israel, while the southern kingdom was known as Judah. Several kings of greatly varying nature ruled the two divisions of the old nation, and the people went through stages of closeness to God followed by periods of severe backsliding.

A little over two-hundred years went by, and the northern kingdom had drifted so far away from God that the Lord's judgment fell upon them. In B.C. 721, the Assyrian army conquered the northern kingdom of Israel.

Judah continued to survive in the south for a little over one-hundred years, then also felt the hand of God's chastisement. In B.C. 606, Nebuchadnezzar, king of Babylon, sent his armies into Judah, and Jerusalem submitted to his rule. At this time many Jews were carried away into captivity. Daniel is thought to have been among this number.

Theologians believe that a period of time is spoken of in the Bible, during which the city of Jerusalem will be ruled over by Gentile power. Christ also spoke of this period of history in the verse of Scripture quoted at the beginning of this chapter. This period of time concerning Gentile supremacy over Jerusalem is known as "The Time of the Gentiles."

Some believe that this time actually began in the year A.D. 70, when Rome sent Titus to stomp out the fires of Jewish rebellion, scattering the Jews throughout the nations of the known world. But at this time, the Jewish nation already had been under Roman rule for over a hundred years. The war ending in A.D. 70 was not a loss of freedom, but the failure of a revolution.

In fact, history shows that from the year B.C. 606, the closest the Jewish nation came to experiencing actual national freedom was in the midst of revolution. Even the years of the Maccabean "kingdom" were at best a prolonged period of treaties for the protection of stronger nations, or rebellion against those nations.

From 606 B.C., to A.D. 70, four main powers held the reigns of authority in the Middle East—Babylon, Medo-Persia, Greco-Macedonia, and Rome. Each Gentile world empire was foretold in the book of Daniel. From A.D. 70, until modern times, no Jewish nation even existed. In view of these facts, the year B.C. 606 appears to be the actual beginning of the Times of the Gentiles as far as national Israel is concerned, for, from that time, until A.D. 1948, the kingdom did not experience unshackled freedom.

The Times of the Gentiles should not be confused with another term appearing in the Bible and also referring to the Gentiles. It is spoken of by Paul in **Romans 11:25,** and is known as the "Fullness of the Gentiles." Whereas the Times of the Gentiles refers to an actual chronological period of time to be measured in years, the Fullness of the Gentiles refers to those people of Gentile origin who are gathered out to be included in the Church. The Church is composed of both Jew and Gentile, but biblical Scripture seems to imply that it will be made up mainly of Gentiles. The foreknowledge of the Lord knows exactly the number of Gentiles that will be included in the Church, and that number in its entirety is the "Fullness of the Gentiles." **Roman 11:25** says that blindness in part is happened to Israel, until the Fullness of the Gentiles is come in. See also, **Acts 15:14.**

The nation of the Jews lost its absolute freedom in B.C. 606, when it surrendered to Babylon. It did not regain that national freedom until many centuries had elapsed—over two and a half millenniums, in fact. In A.D. 1948, the country called Israel was reborn as an independent nation (not a nation to simply represent the northern division of the old kingdom, but a singular nation to represent all twelve tribes.

In theory, the loss of Jewish freedom in B.C. 606 was corrected by the rebirth of the Jewish nation in A.D. 1948—with the exception of the old city of Jerusalem. Therefore, if the period known as the Times of the Gentiles was determined by the national freedom of the Jews, that period ran out in A.D. 1948. This is a period of time totaling 2,553 years. **See Chart 6.**

CHART 6
JEWISH NATIONAL FREEDOM
(Lost and Regained)

```
Babylon                                          Israel
Captivity                                        Reborn
|_____|
B.C. 606            2,553 years            A.D. 1948
```

Babylon extended its rule over the nation of Judah in B.C. 606. The Jewish people did not truly experience national freedom again until the rebirth of Israel in A.D. 1948. This was a period of 2,553 years.

Adam and Eve were the first man and woman of the human race. Being special creations by the hand of God, they were placed in a garden in the land of Eden. Their environmental conditions were perfect. They had beautiful surroundings, ample food, and absence of natural dangers or mortal enemies. Their home was truly a paradise which men have often dreamed of.

But sin entered into that Edenic Garden of Paradise, and Adam and Eve lost the home which they had called their own. Driven out into the world, they found it necessary to bring forth food by the sweat of their faces, battling thorns and thistles in order to harvest a ground that had been cursed. Before the "children" of God would again actually posses a land which they could call their own, an interval of 2,553 years would pass.

While studying this particular span of years, another thing did come to my attention, but I am uncertain whether or not it bears major importance. The value 2,553, when divided by the number thirty-seven, produces the number sixty-nine. Twenty-four of the segments of sixty-nine equal a total of 1,656 years, the exact number of years from the time Adam and Eve were driven from the Garden of Eden until the flood of Noah. However, all attempts to count other intervals in history by using the same sixty-nine year interval has proven completely fruitless. If there is a real lesson in the sixty-nine year periods, perhaps it points out that the Flood was a temporary loss of homeland, in a sense, but was soon replaced by the gift to Noah of the whole world.

In **Chart 7,** I have included the intervals of sixty-nine, marking the Fall in Eden, the flood, and the invasion of Canaan by the children of Israel, led by Joshua. In this figure, a picture of a homeland lost, and a homeland regained is given. Adam and Eve, the children of God, lost their home when they were forced to leave the garden, but the children of God obtained a home when they followed God's leadership into the Promised Land. In the book of Leviticus, written by Moses through divine inspiration, God gives a special warning to his people, that they walk according to his statutes.

CHART 7
THE INTERVALS OF 69 (Approximate Values)

The Fall		The Flood		Promised Land
4004 B.C.	(24 intervals) 1,656 years	2348 B.C.	(13 intervals) 897 years	1451 B.C.
		2,553 years		

According to Usher, Adam and Eve were driven out of the Garden of Eden in B.C. 4004. The Flood occurred in B.C. 2348, a period of 1,656 years after the Fall. This period of time may be divided into 24 intervals of 69 each. Thirteen more of these intervals, counted from the time of the Flood, reaches 897 years later to B.C. 1451. This is the year that the children of Israel entered the Promised Land. The total number of years from B.C. 4004, to B.C. 1451, is 2,553 years.

"And if ye will not for all this hearken unto me, but walk contrary unto me; Then I will walk contrary unto you also in fury; and I, even I, will chastise you seven times for your sins" **(Leviticus 26:27-28).**

Some have interpreted these two verses to refer to seven different but specific periods of chastisement to fall upon the Jews. Others have found in these verses a reference to the seven years of the Tribulation Period, while still others have promoted the theory that the seven "times" mentioned in Leviticus bear a special relationship to the "Times" of the Gentiles, spoken of by Christ in the book of Luke.

"Jerusalem shall be trodden down of the Gentiles, until the times of the Gentiles be fulfilled" (**Luke 21:24**).

In the book of Daniel, the word "times" is used to refer to a portion of the Tribulation Period—*"It shall be for a time, times, and a half."*

In the book of Revelation, this same period of time is denoted as forty-two months. Elsewhere in Revelation, it is designated as 1,260 days. All three terminologies depict a value of about three and a half years. But it is conceivable that the Lord, in his wisdom, has ordained that all three theories be foretold by the Leviticus verses.

Applying the "seven times" to the length of the Times of the Gentiles, an impressive discovery results.

(2,553 divided by 7 equals 364.71428)

This value is remarkably close to another value encountered in the chapter concerning calendars, where it is pointed out that the average basic Jewish calendar year, without special added or subtracted days to coincide the year with the seasons, amounts to 364.68421 days. However, if we attempt to extend the slightly shorter years of the uncorrected Jewish calendar beyond the 2,553-year intervals, nothing really significant seems to appear. So, I have restricted study only to that period of time.

In the prophetic announcement given in the book of Daniel concerning the Seventy weeks, it was found that the time period was to be counted by the scale of "one day equals one year." The Seventy Weeks actually proved to be 490 years. If the Times of the Gentiles is also counted in this manner, each day of the average basic Jewish calendar year would be the equivalent of one "time," as mentioned in Leviticus. Since there are seven times spoken of, the Times of the Gentiles would equal 364.68421 multiplied by seven. The resultant value is 2,552.78947 years.

In B.C. 606, the Babylonian army subdued Jerusalem, but the Jewish culture was allowed to continue for a short time under a Jewish puppet king. Some deportation did occur at that time, but the Jewish state remained largely in tact though under a foreign power. However, a few years later, against the prophetic warnings of Jeremiah the prophet, King Zedekiah elected to resist the authority of Babylon. After an eighteen month siege, Jerusalem fell. The Babylonian army, under the command of Nebuzar-Adan (Nabu-Seri-Idinnam), plundered the city; slaughtered the children of the king, then, put out the eyes of Zedekiah; razed the city walls; deported many Jews out of their homeland; and burned the royal palace and the Temple. The city fell on the ninth day of the fourth month, in B.C. 587, but it was not destroyed until the seventh day of the fifth month. It is the latter of these dates which seems to fulfill the actual words of Christ.

"Jerusalem shall be trodden down of the Gentiles, until the Times of the Gentiles be fulfilled" **(Luke 21:24).**

The words of Christ deal specifically with the city of Jerusalem, not the nation of the Jews. Jerusalem would be in Gentile hands until the Times of the Gentiles be fulfilled. The B.C. 606 date did not fulfill this prophecy in a literal sense, for, even though Jewish national freedom was lost, Jerusalem remained in Jewish hands. However, a definite relationship does seem to exist between national Israel and the times of the Gentiles, since the state was reborn in A.D. 1948, an elapsed time of approximately 2,553 years.

In B.C. 587, nineteen years after the loss of national freedom, the city of Jerusalem was literally trodden down by a Babylonian army.

In A.D. 1967, tensions mounted in the Middle East, as the Arabian-Israeli crisis tightened to the brink of armed conflict. Yielding to the demands of Egyptian President Nassar, United Nations Secretary-General U Thant ordered the withdrawal of peacekeeping U.N. Emergency Forces from the Egyptian-Israeli frontier. Egyptian troops immediately moved into the area and threatened a "hot" war.

On May 22, 1967, President Gamal Nassar closed the gulf of Aqaba to Israeli shipping, and Israel regarded the move as an act of war.

June 5, 1967, war broke out between Israel and the Arab nations. Moving with surprising mobility and strength, Israeli planes caught most of the Arabian air force on the ground and virtually destroyed it. Israeli ground forces stabbed deep into the Sinai Peninsula, completely devastating Egyptian troops in the area. Jewish forces quickly rolled to the banks of the Suez Canal and lifted the blockade of the Gulf of Aqaba.

On the Eastern Front, Israel met with equal success. Against Jordanian forces, Jewish soldiers stormed into the old city of Jerusalem on June 6, 1967. The following day, the ram's horn (shofar) was sounded before the Wailing Wall to proclaim the victory. The ancient city of Jerusalem, connected with the Times of the Gentiles, was once in Jewish hands.

These happened nineteen years after the state of Israel was reborn as a nation, and 2,553 years after the city had been trodden down in B.C. 587. Using the basic Jewish calendar to determine the times of the Gentiles, and counting back from the modern June 6, 1967 date, the results are as follows.

2552.78947 (Times of the Gentiles)
minus 1966.42959 (June 6, 1957 A.D.)
equals 586.35988 B.C.

The date is the 234th day of the year, or August 22, B.C. 587. The city and Temple were destroyed on the seventh day of the fifth month in the Jewish calendar. This roughly corresponds with the month of August, the exact alignment depending upon the particulars year's position in the Jewish 19-year cycle (see the chapter covering calendars, and, **Chart 8.**

CHART 8
JERUSALEM AND THE TIMES OF THE GENTILES

Jerusalem Destroyed	Jerusalem Regained
586.35988 B.C.	1966.42959 A.D.
(August 22, B.C. 587)	(June 6, A.D. 1967)
	2,553 years

The Times of the Gentiles, as pointed out by Christ, was measured by the captivity of Jerusalem. As shown in this chapter, the Times of the Gentiles seems to have ran out on June 6, A.D. 1967.

These figures seem to verify the theory that the Times of the Gentile truly ran out in A.D. 1967, another sign substantiating the nearness of the Lord's Second coming! For those who scoff at the idea that things which happened in the days described in the Old Testament have any connection with our modern age, the study of the 2,553 years seems to prove their scoffing in error.

The same God who revealed the future to the prophets of old was the same person who was born into the world just over 2,000 years ago. The same Lord who formed the planet we live on, also formed the heavens, then died upon a humble cross to buy back the souls of men who had forsaken and despised him. He spoke the words that lay down the boundaries of the Time of the Gentiles, then brought them to pass. He also rose victorious from the tomb, then ascended into the glory of his heavens, but, before leaving, left behind a promise that he would return. There is no doubt that he will keep that promise and arrive back at exactly the time appointed. These things were planned before the first atom was incorporated into the structure of the earth, for the true God of the Bible is God, and is alive today!

On the other hand, if the Times of the Gentiles ended in A.D. 1967, what of the reference made in **Revelation 11:2,** which is in the future? Many have believed that the Times of the Gentiles will not end until the Lord's return at the close of the Tribulation Period. But the words spoken by Christ **(Luke 21:24)** and the things that happened in 1967 are too similar to be disregarded. All prophetic requirements actually concerning the Times of the Gentiles have been fulfilled in the results of the Six-Day War, leading to the conclusion that this time did run out in that year.

So, the period of time spoken of in the first part of the eleventh chapter of Revelation must be a second "Times of the Gentiles," just as the 70-year exile of the Jews in Daniel's time is separate from the long centuries of exile which began in the year, A.D. 70. The length of the Second Times of the Gentiles is plainly told in Scripture.

"But the court which is without the temple leave out, and measure it not; for it is given unto the Gentiles: and the holy city shall they tread under foot forty and two months" **(Revelation 11:2).**

There is no mystery about this period of time. The verse following, speaking of the ministry of the two witnesses and the length of their prophesying, make it evident that time is the last half of the Tribulation Period. It is forty-two months long, or 1,260 days, or three and a half years. It is also synonymous with the length of time associated with the woman of Revelation 12. The woman in this chapter represents Israel. Satan, who has been cast out of heaven in the midst of the Tribulation Period, seeks to persecute the Jewish people through the beast—the Antichrist.

"And there was war in heaven: Michael and his angels fought against the dragon; and the dragon fought with his angels, And prevailed not; neither was their place found any more in heaven, and the great dragon was cast out, that old serpent, called the Devil, and Satan, which deceiveth the whole world: he was cast out into the earth, and his angels were cast out with him" **(Revelation 12:7-9).**

In these verses, Satan experiences his second fall from the heights of heaven. In **Luke 10:18,** Jesus declares to his followers that he *"beheld Satan as lightning fall from heaven."* Christ was speaking of an incident which occurred thousands of years before history, when Satan was defeated in his rebellion against God. But, from that time, the devil has been allowed to venture before the throne of the Lord where he has persisted day and night in bringing accusations against the children of the Lord yet residing upon the earth **(Job 1:6-12; Revelation 12:10b).** Now, in the midst of the Tribulation Period, Satan has been cast out of heaven and arrives in person upon the earth, seeking revenge through the Antichrist against the Jewish people.

Why do you suppose Satan has been so persistent in his hatred of the children of Jacob through the centuries, even in the 1,878 years from A.D. 70, when they were not a nation? Even now, Israel cannot be regarded as one of the more powerful nations on earth, so probably could not be considered as a reliable means for Satan to achieve world domination. The hatred of Satan for Christians can be understood, and, among the ranks of Christianity there are many of Jewish heritage, but since Israel, as a nation, has not yet recognized Jesus as the actual Messiah, the sacrificial lamb who came into the world to lay down his own life at Passover to cleanse away all sin, where is his motive?

When the promise of a Messiah was first made, it was to Adam and Eve in the Garden of Eden, when God confronted them concerning the transgression they had committed. I do not know how well they understood exactly what the coming of Messiah would accomplish, but I do believe I can perceive what was primary in their hearts at that time. They surely longed for the lost fellowship with God to be restored in its fullness, and to be cleansed of the sin for which they has been found guilty.

Why did the children of Israel fail to recognize the Messiah when he came to them almost two-thousand years ago? Many did, but most did not. Unlike Adam and Eve, they looked for a deliverer to loose them from the enforced bondage they had endured under the Roman government. They longed for the freedom of their nation, and had forgotten the original reason a Messiah was to be given to them. In America, we sometimes have difficulty in comprehending the mind of those in bondage, for most of us have generations of freedom behind us. But, in the same situation, we would certainly have been filled with a huge longing to be free, just as they did, and it would take a special insight to see the truth.

Satan does not posses foreknowledge as does God, but he does posses great intelligence, and he was aware of the prophecies concerning the Messiah. I am very confident that he suspected Christ would be born of the Jewish race, so he attempted to purge them from the world. However, having failed to prevent the birth of the Savior or to keep Christ from laying down his life on the Cross, he now pursues a policy of revenge upon the race of people he holds responsible for his own defeat, for the Jews brought Jesus of Nazareth into the world. They also brought to us the oracles of God, which have been accumulated into one all-important book called the Bible. *"What advantage then hath the Jew? or what profit is there of circumcision? Much in every way; because that unto them were committed the oracles of God"* **(Romans 3:1-2).** It should also be pointed out that Jesus, himself, was ***"THE WORD OF GOD!"***

In addition to the revenge attitude of Satan, it has also been pointed out that Satan's war against the Jewish race may include an alternate scheme running parallel to the other. The Bible contains abundant promises concerning the Jews, their nation, and future prominence. **"If"** he could actually succeed in eliminating them from existence, it would be impossible for God to fulfill those promises., and might mean that Satan (since such a failure of God would show that God was not perfect) might mean that God would have to forgive the devil for also being less than perfect.

It is a pity that the very people "chosen" to bring about the birth of the Messiah, should now find themselves the object of so much persecution (instigated by Satan) down through the centuries of the last two millennia. But it will not be so forever, for Paul tells us that *"blindness in part is happened to Israel, until the Fulness of the Gentiles be come in."* Somewhere, near the close of the seven years of the Tribulation, the Jewish nation will at last turn to Jesus, fully recognizing him as the Anointed One of God, the long-awaited one called the Messiah. Then, the Lord Jesus will return to defend them, and put down their persecutors—and establish his kingdom.

When we think of the mother of Jesus, we always think of Mary. But, in reality, Israel bore the Messiah, Mary being the individual proxy through which the birth was accomplished. The Jewish people were and still remain the "chosen race," but we sometimes forget just what that means. Through the descendants of Abraham, Isaac, and Jacob the blessing of Messiah came into the world. Israel is referred to in the Old Testament as the wife of Jehovah, and that "marriage" brought forth the Son of God which would take away the sins of the world.

"And the woman fled into the wilderness, where she hath a place prepared of God, that they should feed her there a thousand two hundred and threescore days" (**Revelation 12:6**).

The Second Time of the Gentiles is the series of events Christ speaks of in **Matthew 24:15-22,** when he refers to the *"abomination of desolation,"* and the need for desperate flight (also referred to in **Daniel 9:27**). The Second Times of the Gentiles will be concluded when the Lord Jesus Christ returns to the earth at the close of the Tribulation Period as *"King of Kings, and Lord of Lords."*

THE SEVENTY YEARS

In the study of the 2,553 years, there is another interval of time which did play a part in the prophecies concerning the Babylonian invasion and the destruction of Jerusalem and the temple. I honestly do not know if it should also be included in the modern history of Israel and Jerusalem—but I suspect it probably is. Apparently, it was not included in the very first occurrence of the 2,553-year interval, which spanned the time between Adam and Eve's Fall in the Garden of Eden and the entrance of the Hebrews, led by Joshua, into the Promised Land. The special interval is a period of seventy years.

Daniel was aware of it, for he writes, *"In the first year of Darius the son of Ahasureus, of the seed of the Medes, which was made king over the realm of the Chaldeans; In the first year of his reign I Daniel understood by books the number of the years whereof the word of the Lord came to Jeremiah the prophet, that he would accomplish seventy years in the desolations of Jerusalem"* **(Daniel 9:1-2)**.

Daniel was a student of the books written by Jeremiah, and he was aware of the relationship of Jeremiah's prophetic works to the time in which Daniel lived. Jeremiah wrote, *"And this whole land shall be a desolation, and an astonishment; and these nations shall serve the king of Babylon seventy years"* **(Jeremiah 25:11)**. The prophet also wrote, *"or thus saith the Lord, That after seventy years be accomplish at Babylon I will visit you, and perform my good word toward you, in causing you to return to this place"* **(Jeremiah 29:10)**.

This seventy-year interval did take place, and, the seventy years of exile were counted from the time when the Babylonian army conquered Jerusalem (B.C. 606), but not from the time, nineteen years later, when the army came to squash the Jewish rebellion, and stayed to destroy the city and the temple (B.C. 587).

So, the seventy-year interval covered the number of years from B.C. 606, to B.C. 536. If the seventy-year interval, given at the time of Babylon's venture into Jerusalem, is a valid part of the modern span of 2,553 years pointing to both the rebirth of Israel as a nation and to the acquisition of the old city of Jerusalem, to agree with the first application, that value would have to be counted from the rebirth of Israel as a nation, or, A.D. 1948. This points to a year somewhat further into the future that some would like to believe, namely, A.D. 2018. But, the actual merit of the date would depend very highly upon just what the date might represent in the unfolding of eschatology.

I do feel confident in saying, "if" the interval is meant to be placed in the manner I have just shown in the above paragraph, it is **NOT** to be used to designate the year of the Rapture of the Church! That is a day not revealed to us—at least, I know it has not been revealed to me and I feel the exact day will not be revealed to others before it happens. But, most Christians who believe in the Rapture of the Church do agree that the time is not very far into the future, and is surely growing closer every day. However, it is generally believed that "signs" are given mainly for the benefit of the Jews, and, since all of the dates and times in the 2,553-year intervals are dates concerning the Jewish nation, I can only surmise that the modern interval of seventy years, if it is to be applied, also points to an important event in the Jewish world.

What happened in the year, B.C. 536? The Bible tells us that a certain number of Jewish people went back to Jerusalem. The reason for that return is given in II Chronicles and Ezra.

ANow in the first year of Cyrus king of Persia, that the word of the Lord spoken by the mouth of Jeremiah might be accomplished, the Lord stirred up the spirit of Cyrus king of Persia, that he made a proclamation throughout all his kingdom, and put it in writing, saying, Thus saith Cyrus king of Persia, All the kingdoms of the earth hath the Lord God of Heaven given me, and he hath charged me to build him an house in Jerusalem, which is in Judah. Who is there among you of all his people? The Lord God be with him, and let him go up" **(II Chronicles 36:22-23).**

The book of Ezra begins with almost the same words as quoted above, and continues the story from that point. According to **Ezra 2:64-65,** a fairly large company of Jews returned to Jerusalem—almost 50,000 individuals in all. Two men stood up to lead them. They were

Jeshua (the Hebrew form of the Greek name Jesus) and Zerubbabel. The first official act of this congregation was to build *"The altar of the God of Israel,"* and *"To offer burnt-offerings thereon, as it is written in the law of Moses the man of God"* **(Ezra 3:2).** The reason for their return to Jerusalem was to rebuild the Temple!

We know that there will be a great temple in existence during the Golden Millennium. We know that the city of Jerusalem will be constructed, along with the home of the great King Jesus, from which he will rule over the established kingdoms of the world for one-thousand years. "If" the seventy-year interval truly is to be applied in our age, A.D. 2018 could be the year in which the order is proclaimed to begin the building.

We also must remember that such a task would be begun only after the Lord Jesus has returned to the earth at the close of the Tribulation Period, and, after certain other necessary things have taken place— namely, the Battle of Armageddon, the casting of the Antichrist and the False Prophet into the Lake of Fire, the temporary imprisonment of Satan, emergency provisions and care for the earth's remaining population, and the Judgment of the Nations to determine which nations shall, or shall not, continue on into the Millennial Kingdom. How much time these individual acts may consume is unknown to me.

The duration of the Tribulation period is, of course, seven years, but whether or not there will be an undetermined span of time between the Rapture of the Church and the beginning of the seven years, I do not know with certainty. Some very reputable theologians think there may be. Even so, I do not expect the northern kingdom's invasion into the Middle-East, should it occur before, during, or after the Church is taken out of the world, to use up very much time, for the Bible seems to portray a quick and decisive termination of that endeavor. The rise of Antichrist to power could take a little longer, unless he already holds a very high place in the world's eye at the time of the Rapture.

Without knowing with great surety that the seventy-year span of time is to be projected forward to the year, A.D. 2018, I will leave it to the reader's own convictions to make that decision. I know what I quietly believe in the privacy of my own heart, but that should not persuade others. The Holy Spirit of the Lord remains the only reliable source of enlightenment in such matters.

The two periods of 2,553 years, tying together the events of the Babylonian conquest of the Jewish land 600 years before the birth of Christ, with the twentieth-century rebirth of Israel and the Jewish renewed ownership of the ancient city of Jerusalem, are matters that have already come to pass. The problem of trying to predict dates still in the future is another matter. I will leave it up to the reader to form his own opinion concerning the seventy years, and to estimate just how near the Rapture may actually be drawing to us. In **Chart 9** we are shown the measurements of the 2,553-year periods, along with the seventy-year intervals.

CHART 9
THE 2,553-YEAR INTERVALS AND THE 70-YEAR INTERVALS

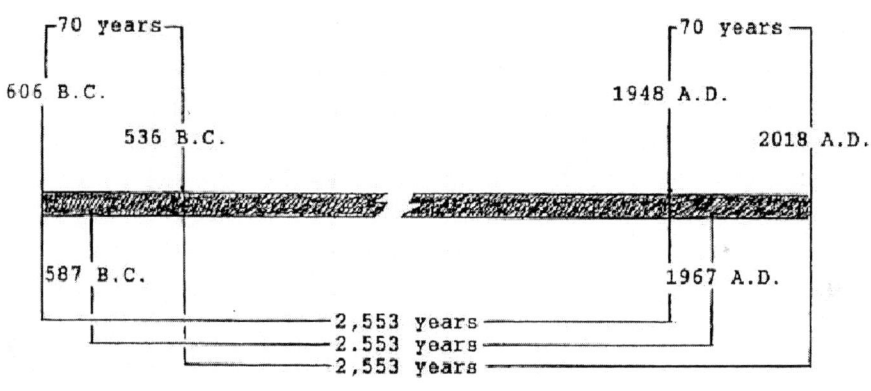

Supplement to Chapter 9

"Now all these things happened to them for ensamples: and they are written for our admonition, upon whom the ends of the world are come" **(1 Corinthians 10:11).**

"For whatsoever things were written aforetime were written for our learning, that we patient through patience and comfort of the Scriptures might have hope" (**Romans 15:4**).

In different locations in this work, reference is made to the possibility that, after the Rapture of the Church, the rise of Antichrist to world power might require an unknown period of time (perhaps from one to two years) before the signing of this pact to mark the beginning of time generally referred to as the Tribulation Period **(Matthew 24:21; Revelation 7:14)**, or, the Time of Jacob's Trouble **(Jeremiah 30:7)**, or, the last week of Daniel's Seventy Weeks **(Daniel 9:24-27)**.

I also pointed out that a list of several events following the visible return of Christ to the world, at the close of the Tribulation Period, might require a little longer time to unfold than some may have expected. I have included this supplement to explain why I suggested those theories in the text.

If we accept the 70-year Interval, mentioned in this chapter, as a legitimate length of time to be counted from the year of Israel's Rebirth as a nation in A.D. 1948, we have seen that the particular span of years points to A.D. 2018. In theory, we compared the "happening" at the end of the 70-year period bridging the border between the 20th and 21st centuries, and concluded that the event at the end of that period "could" be the proclamation (personally given by the Lord Jesus Christ) to begin building the Millennial Temple and the city of Jerusalem. If this is true, what transpires between the present date and A.D. 2018? The following is a list of events which must happen from the Rapture to the command to begin building the Temple and the millennial capital.

1. The Rapture of the Church.
2. The Invasion of the Middle-East by Russia.
3. The Rising to power by the Antichrist
4. The Seven-year Tribulation Period.
5. The Return of Christ to the world.
6. The Battle of Armageddon.
7. Antichrist and the False Prophet cast into the Lake of Fire.

8. A system established to provide for the needs of the world's population.
9. The Judgment of the Nations.
10. The Commandment to build the Temple and Jerusalem.

Other than the Rapture of the Church, which transpires in the "twinkling of an eye," and the seven years of the tribulation, the other happenings on the list are of an unknown duration. Some may require only a short span of time while others may unfold over a longer period. Following are some estimations I have made exploring what I consider to be the shortest scenario reasonably possible, and, a second scenario that unfolds over a more lengthy interval.

TWO POSSIBLE SCENARIOS:

(1) If the first three events described above unfold in very rapid order (or if the Antichrist is already in power when the first two events happen and they are very short in transpiring), the seven years of the Tribulation Period could begin very soon after the rescue of the Church out of the world. That would leave only three events between the return of Christ to the earth at the close of the tribulation, and the command to rebuild the Temple. If these things can take place in the space of just one year, we only have to subtract eight years from A.D. 2018, and we have the year A.D. 2010, which, would seem to be the last possible year for the Rapture, "if" the 70-year period is to be counted in our age.

(2) (2) The longer of the two scenarios is based upon certain information given to us directly from the pages of the Bible, but not necessarily recognized by most people as useful in predicting the "end days." However, these things are accepted by many as granting us a glimpse of the last days through examples or types. Christ once referred to one of the "examples" when he warned us of the days of Noah.

"But as the days of Noe [Noah] were, so shall also the coming of the Son of man be" **(Matthew 24:37).**

Many students of the Bible limit these particular words to the style of life that will be dominant in the latter years just before Christ returns. But Christ continued to point out that *"The days of Noah"* are to considered *"The days that were before the flood"* **(:38),** and, in this sense, might also include the entire series of events reaching all the way back to Adam. Christ speaks of the natural happenings of life—people living and planning, eating, drinking, and marrying. But their plans did not include God!

All of us plan for the future as though we will be around to enjoy it, and it is not wrong to do so. We invest in insurance policies to guard against sickness and to help our survivors in the event of our demise, and, certainly, no one would condemn us for taking that precaution. But, many of those who are careful about these things leave the greatest and most needed insurance policy completely out of their plans—the truth and assurance that you belong to Christ Jesus, and, no matter what may happen in the world, the knowledge that you are eternally safe and covered in the shelter of His grace! The world of the Alast days' will have greatly forgotten this, and, this very oversight was one of the truths that Jesus pointed out to his disciples—and to us.

An account of events between the Fall of Adam and the Flood also gives us a remarkable picture corresponding with certain very significant things which will come to pass in the days before the return of the Lord to the earth.

The Last Days are also referred to as the Days of Apostasy, when the world in general will abandon true faith in God, and heap to itself false doctrine and false religion. Such crops of Godlessness always plunge the harvester into depths of total debauchery, and result in ultimate doom. These conditions will be prevalent upon the world during the Last Days, as they were also prevalent in the days before the coming of the Flood.

*"And Enoch walked with God: and he was not; for God took him" (***Genesis 5:24).**

"By faith Enoch was translated that he should not see death; and was not found, because God had translated him: for before his translation he had this testimony, that he pleased God" **(Hebrews 11:5).**

The sixth chapter of Genesis describes the conditions between the Rapture of Enoch and the punishment of the Flood. Following the departure of Enoch from the world, the generations of mankind quickly fell away from the truth of God. Following the departure of the Church from the world, mankind will once again fall before the wiles of Satan and choose for themselves a leader whom the Bible refers to as the Antichrist.

That the period of time between the Translation of Enoch and the Flood is in truth a picture of the years between the Rapture of the Church and the Return of Christ is further shown by the number of years attributed to that time by the book of Genesis. The value is 669 years (discussed in chapter eleven of this book), a symbolism pointing to the number of the Antichrist **(Revelation 13:18)** with the third six inverted. Enoch's translation shows us the Rapture of the Church, while the Flood shows us the judgment of the Lord Jesus Christ falling upon the armies of the world at the Battle of Armageddon. The years which are between represent the rise of Antichrist and the Tribulation.

The Bible also tells us of another man whose life seems to give us a remarkable representation of the Rapture and the Return of Christ. His name was Joseph, and his story is well known to almost all people having a passing knowledge of Old Testament personages. Children learn in Sunday School of his coat of many colors and that he was an interpreter of dreams. One of the sons of the patriarch Jacob, he became the father of one of the twelve tribes of Israel, but not before he was betrayed by his brethren and sold into slavery, from which he eventually rose to power and position in the greatest nation of his time.

Jacob did not hide the fact that Joseph was his favorite son, which caused his older brothers to resent him. Shortly after Joseph became seventeen years old, his jealous brothers discovered a chance to rid themselves of their hated kinsman. In a distant pasture far from home, they conspired to sell him into bondage, and a Midianite caravan carried him into Egypt where he was sold as a slave.

The Bible tells us that he quickly rose in the eyes of his owner and was given authority over his owner's possessions. The scorned wife of the owner caused him to be cast into prison, but the Lord of Heaven did not forget Joseph!

A chain of event brought him out of prison and placed him before the king of Egypt, where he interpreted the king's dream. He warned of seven good years of harvest, followed by seven bad years. He advised that a good man should be sought out who would supervise the project of laying up a portion of the good years of harvest to use during the seven bad years. The king of Egypt was so pleased with Joseph's plan that he chose him to be the man over that project, and elevated him to the position of ruler of Egypt, second only to the king. Joseph married a gentile bride, and was eventually reunited with his family.

Joseph was 17-years old when he was sold into slavery, and was placed in prison when he was 28-years old. He was released from prison at 30, elevated to a high office, and married soon after. He was reunited with his brethren when he was 39-years old.

Many students of the Bible see a very strong picture in the story of Joseph's life, presenting to us a "type" of things to occur during the last days before the Millennial Kingdom. For instance, his release from prison typifies the Rapture of the church, for it is certainly a release both from the bonds of the sinful world and from the bonds of mortal flesh. Joseph is bathed and cleansed, then stands before the king of Egypt; the Church will also be cleansed and clothed in robes of white as they stand before the King of all Creation. Joseph married a gentile bride; the Church participates in the marriage of the Lamb. A terrible famine came upon the land of Joseph's day; the tribulation will come upon the world after the Church has been taken out. After a few years, Joseph was reunited with his brethren, while when Christ returns to the earth after the Tribulation Period, he will be reunited with his brethren, the Jewish people.

It appears that the accounts of Joseph and the days before the flood of Noah's time both offer a picture or type of the time preceding the return of Christ to the earth. Both show an example of the Rapture of the Church, and both show a symbolism of things that will occur shortly after the visible return of Christ to the Mount of Olives. Thereof, it would seem only reasonable that the two accounts bear a resemblance in their sizes or structures. That resemblance does exists.

An examination of the first 39 years of Joseph's life shows a definite division into certain main segments. There were 17 years from his birth to his betrayal into slavery; 13 years from his betrayal to his rescue from prison; and 9 years from the rescue to his thirty-ninth year, when he was reunited with his brethren.

Between the Fall of Adam in the Garden of Eden and the flood of Noah's day there were 1,656 years. Although the Bible does not give great detail concerning individual events happening during this lengthy period of time, the births and deaths of the ancestry of Christ are presented. We know that, from the Fall of Adam in the garden to the Translation of Enoch, there were 987 year, and, from the Translation of Enoch to the Flood there were 669 years. If charts representing the systems of Joseph and Noah, scaled to comparable lengths, are laid side by side, it is apparent that the charts harmonize in their divisions. If the Fall of Adam is placed next to the betrayal of Joseph, and the Flood is lined up with the reuniting of Joseph with his brethren, the release of Joseph from prison lines up quite well with the Rapture of Enoch. See **Chart 10.**

James F. Webb

CHART 10
COMPARISON OF THE THIRTY-NINE YEARS OF JOSEPH WITH THE DAYS OF NOAH

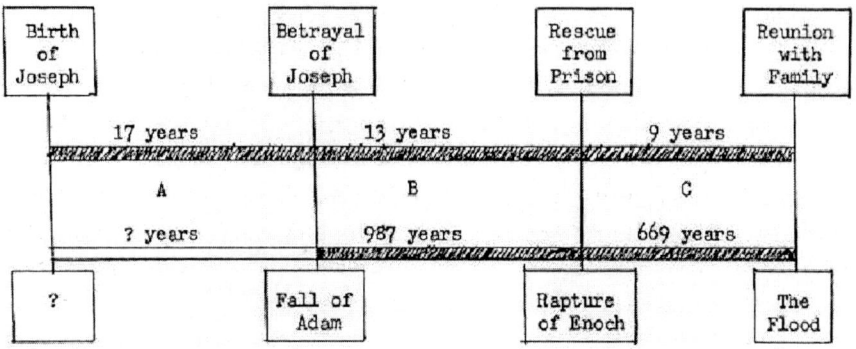

The first 39 years of Joseph's life are laid out for comparison beside the Days of Noah (period of time between the Fall in the Garden of Eden and the Flood), with the appropriate alignments made. Allowing for the fact that individual dates of the year are not available for every event, the rounded values of the segments do seem to be proportionate. An exact value for Segment A in the Days of Noah is not given in the Book of Genesis. The segments presented in this illustration are not drawn to exact scale, but number values are from the Bible.

In this figure, the Thirty-nine Years of Joseph and the Days of Noah are demonstrated next to one another. The three main segments of the two systems are designated by the letters A, B, and C. Although the figure is not drawn to scale, the numeric values of the systems are accurate and may be compared. Simple mathematics show that the corresponding lengths of B and C are indeed proportionate.

Following are actual mathematical ratios existing between segments B and C, keeping in mind that the comparisons are made using round-year values without respect to months or portions of years.

Cross Ratio.....Segment B............987 divided by 13 = 75.9
Cross Ratio.....Segment C............669 divided by 9 = 74.3

Inter Ratio ......Days of Noah ....987 divided by   669 = 1.47
Inter Ratio ......39-Years/Joseph.... .13 divided by   9 = 1.44

Some may notice that Segment A gives a value of 17 years for the layout representing Joseph's life, but no corresponding value is given in the layout for the Days of Noah. It seems probable that the event lining up with the birth of Joseph might be the creation of Adam, but the Bible records no intervals of time or dates covering that period. If the reader wants to calculate on his own, it is simple to fill in a value for that segment, using the ratios given in the other two segments.

I did notice that the segments of Joseph's first thirty-nine years do follow a special pattern—each segment differing from the segment touching it by four years. That is, Segment B is four years longer than Segment C, while Segment A is four years longer than Segment B. If the same method is used in the Days of Noah chart, you will arrive at a mathematical value which will fall in the second half of the sixth Great Day of the Creation Week. This does correspond with what the Bible tells us about the creation of Adam, regardless of the actual length of those days.

If the 70 years "are" to be added to the modern birth of Israel, and the year, A.D. 2018, "is" actually the Lord's command to begin construction of the Millennial Temple and the city of Jerusalem, how does **Chart 10** help us to understand the number of years before this date?

In the Bible's account of the life of Joseph, three other time periods are pointed out with enough information supplied to enable us to place them un the figure with a degree of accuracy. At the age of twenty-eight, Joseph was placed in prison. He was released about two years later at the age of thirty. He predicts the seven years of good harvests followed by the seven years of bad harvests. At the age of thirty-nine, he is reunited with his own family. This is nine years after his release from prison, and, if the good years began at that time, he would have been joined with his brethren two years into the time of bad harvests.

Joseph sent a special message to his Father.

"And thou shalt dwell in the land of Goshen, and thou shalt be near unto me, thou, and thy children, and thy children's children, and thy flocks, and thy herds, and all that thou hast: And there I will nourish thee; for yet there are five years of famine" **(Genesis 45:10-11a).**

I have used all this information to form the second Scenario attempting to make a very crude estimate concerning the things which take place between the Rapture os the Church and the crude estimate concerning the things which take place between the Rapture of the Church and the order to began building the Millennial Temple.

We know, according to Joseph's life, that he was reunited with his family nine years after he was released from prison. If this joyous reunion presents a picture of the period between the Rapture and the Second Coming of Christ, it seems to lend some credence to the thought that it might take as much as two years for the Antichrist to rise to complete power and form the seven-year covenant with Israel. And, "if" the words of Joseph in Genesis 45:11a, may be applied after the return of Jesus, it "could" mean a period of time between the Return of Christ and the start of construction on the temple—as much as five years.

So what are my conclusions? Though we cannot place a definite date upon the Rapture, in my opinion, based upon the two studies we have just finished, it "could" fall anywhere from A.D. 2004, through A.D. 2010. Perhaps, due to the desire in my heart and certain other factors, I do lean toward the earlier year.

Concerning the other factors: I have found that, if A.D. 30 is the beginning of the Church Age, and, if that age ends in A.D. 2004 (if that should be the year of the Rapture), then the years of the Church Age would be 1,974 years long. In the Days of Noah, the period from the Fall of Adam to the Rapture of Enoch is 987-years long. It is interesting that, if we divide 1,974 by 2, the answer is 987!

Comparing the 9-year interval from the years of Joseph with the 669-year interval from the Days of Noah, we find that 669 divided by 9 equals 74.333. If we convert 669 to 666 and divide by 9 the result is 74 even. Also, if the first 39 years of Joseph's life, from birth to reunion with his family, plus the additional 5 years mentioned by

Joseph to the end of the famine, are subtracted from the modern year, A.D. 2018, the result is the year, A.D. 1974.

(It may or may not be of significance that in October, 1974, Yasir Arafat, at the Rabat summit meeting of Arab states, was able to persuade the Arab nations to accept the Palestine Liberation Organization (PLO) as the only representative of the Palestinian people. In November, the United Nations greeted Yasir Arafat, a known terrorist, with a standing ovation and greatly elevated the prominence of the PLO by bestowing upon it the official honor of observer status.)

And, if 9 (segment C from the Joseph chart) is multiplied times 669 (segment C from the Noah chart) the result is 6,021. If we subtract 4,004 (the year of Adam and Eve's expulsion from the garden) from 6,021 (and add 1 additional year to allow for the fact that there is no zero year between B.C. 1, and A.D. 1), the result is 2018! What the chances are that these several intervals and numbers from the Bible and modern history could work out the way I have just shown, I will leave to mathematicians. However, there are other comparisons that should be considered to raise the number of chances even higher.

There are sixty-six books in the Bible. The Old Testament contains thirty-nine, while the New Testament contains twenty-seven. It does not take much observant thought to notice that these numbers exhibit the same proportions found in the intervals used from the life of Joseph. Thirty-nine divided by three equals thirteen; and, twenty-seven divided by three equals nine. It would seem that the construction of the Bible itself points us to Joseph and the Days of Noah.

Also, the book of the prophet Isaiah contains sixty-six books. Many years ago, Rev. C.I. Scofield, D.D., pointed out that the book is divided into two theoretical parts, assigning the first thirty-nine chapters to before the exile and the last twenty-seven chapters to after.

Here are two quotes from that very book of the Bible.

"Let them bring them forth, and shew us what shall happen: let them shew the former things, what they be, that we may consider them, and know the latter end of them; or declare us things for to come" **(Isaiah 41:22).**

"Remember the former things of old: for I am God, and there is none else; for I am God, and there is none like me, declaring the end from the beginning, and from ancient times the things that are not yet done, saying, My counsel shall stand, and I will do all my pleasure" **(Isaiah 46:9-10).**

Of course, we cannot prove with surety that the thirty-nine years of Joseph are to be counted as normal years. Perhaps, though the duration of the segments do compliment one another in their proportions, they are not to be counted as years of 365 days as in our calendar. So, based simply upon the story of Joseph, I cannot guarantee that the Rapture of the Church is other than simply very near. If the years of Joseph "are" to counted as literal years, then the Lord will return for the Church very soon indeed! If the 70-year period is to be counted from the year A.D. 1948, that fact in itself should be considered as the clear blast of a trumpet, warning that God is still working in the affairs of the world, and that He is coming! So, I do look for him to come for the Church not later than A.D. 2010, but, in my heart I lean to the earlier year of 2004.

I have not taken the studies I have presented in this book lightly. I am aware that most people, today, will be inclined not believe them, but, they are in the Bible, and may be reviewed by anyone who desires to do so. I have treated them as road signs along the highway of life, which present information we are usually inclined to accept. But, sometimes, we read them and misinterpret what they tell us.

Though the window I present to the public is that I look for the Lord to return from 2004 A.D. to 2010 A.D., I would not be surprised if he came tomorrow.

Chapter 10
The Rapture of the Church

"And if I go and prepare a place for you, I will come again, and receive you unto myself, that where I am, there ye may be also" **(John 14:3).**

Many Christians believe that a remarkable event will soon take place involving the Church. Nothing completely like it has ever happened in this world before—at least no happening so magnificent on a scale of such magnitude. As far as the world is concerned, millions of people of all ages, nationalities, and races, will simply disappear without a physical trace as to what happened to them. It will be as though they existed one second, then, did not exist the next second. *"In the twinkling of an eye,"* the Apostle Paul tells us, *"we shall all be changed."* Of course, those who "disappear" and are "changed" will know exactly what has happened to them, for it has been foretold for at least two-thousand years. The remarkable event is the Rapture of the Church.

"Let not your heart be troubled: ye believe in God, believe also in me. In my Father's house are many mansions: if it were not so, I would have told you. I go to prepare a place for you. And if I go and prepare a place for you, I will come again, and receive you unto myself; that where I am, there ye may be also" **(John 14:1-3).**

There are other Scriptures which tell about the Rapture.

"Behold, I show you a mystery; We shall not all sleep, but we shall all be changed, in a moment, in the twinkling of an eye, at the last trump; for the trumpet shall sound, and the dead shall be raised incorruptible, and we shall be changed. For this corruptible must put on incorruption, and this mortal must put on immortality" **(I Corinthians 15:51-53).**

"But I would not have you to be ignorant, brethren, concerning them which are asleep, that ye sorrow not, even as others which have no hope. For if we believe that Jesus died and rose again, even so them also which sleep in Jesus will God bring with him. For this we

say unto you by the word of the Lord, that we which are alive and remain unto the coming of the Lord shall not prevent them which are asleep. For the Lord himself shall descend from heaven with a shout, with the voice of the archangel, and the trump of God; and the dead in Christ shall rise first, then we which are alive and remain shall be caught up together with them in the clouds, to meet the Lord in the air; and so shall we ever be with the Lord:" **(I Thessalonians 4:13-17).**

The Rapture is the "blessed hope" of the Church **(Titus 4:13-17)**, and the moment in time when Christians lay aside the cares and troubles of this world, and physically go to live forever with the Lord Jesus. Although the word "Rapture" does not actually appear in the English translation of the Bible, I am told that the root word from which "rapture" is derived is found in the original Greek versions. In English translations of the Bible, the word is usually written "translated," or "caught away," from the Latin word, raptus, or raptius, or rapere. But popular word of mouth usage has adopted the modern form of the old word because of its meaning. Webster defines "rapture" as the "state of being carried away with joy, love, etc.; ecstasy." what better word could be chosen to refer to such a glorious happening!

There are differences of opinion concerning when the Rapture will occur. Separate theologies may be found which refer to the Rapture taking place either Pre-Tribulation, Mid-Tribulation, or Post-Tribulation. That is, some believe that the Rapture will transpire before the Tribulation Period, some at a point mid-way through the seven-year period, while others hold that it will happen at the close of the period of great Tribulation. The latter opinion is apparently based upon the verses of Scripture found in the twenty-fourth chapter of Matthew, where is described a certain gathering together at the close of the seven years of tribulation.

"Immediately after the tribulation of those days shall the sun be darkened, and the moon shall not give her light, and the stars shall fall from heaven, and the powers of the heavens shall be shaken: and then shall appear the sign of the Son of man in heaven, and then shall all the tribes of the earth mourn, and they shall see the Son of man coming in the clouds of heaven with power and great glory. and he

shall send his angels with a great sound of a trumpet, and they shall gather together his elect from the four winds, from one end of heaven to the other" **(Matthew 24:29-31)**.

It is clear that these events do occur at the close of the Tribulation Period. In fact, it would appear that most of the verses in the remainder of chapter twenty-four also take place as the seven-year period draws to a close. But they do not refer to the Rapture of the Church. When Christ returns to take the Church out, the world will not see him nor be aware that he has visited the earth, at least, not until it is all over. But in the above verses, they do witness him and are filled with dread.

In the verses following those quoted above, Jesus speaks a parable of the fig tree, and, it seems apparent that it is given in relation to the verses coming immediately before it. In the parable he says, *"When his branch is yet tender, and putteth forth leaves, ye know that summer is nigh: So likewise ye, when ye shall see all these things, know that it is near, even at the doors. Verily, I say unto you, This generation shall not pass, till all these things be fulfilled."*

The parable of the fig tree counts times all the way to the Return of the Lord at the close of the Tribulation. the "day" referred to in verse thirty-six speaks of that same event—the Second Coming. The well-known verses showing two in the field and two at the mill, where one of each pair is taken and the other left, is often used to picture the Rapture, and, in many ways, there surely is a similarity. But, in context, the actual verses seem to be a continuation of verse thirty-one, where angels are sent to gather together the yet living saved of the earth (those who did not accept the mark of the beast or bow to him). These are joined with Christ and the redeemed who have returned to the world from heaven, that they might view but be protected from what is to follow—the battle of Armageddon.

The Rapture of the Church will take place before the seven years of the Tribulation Period begin. Paul assures us of this as he writes in the fifth chapter of I Thessalonians, where he has just spoken of the terrible things to befall those on the earth who have rejected him. But he says to the Christians, that "God hath not appointed us to wrath."

The are other familiar "pictures" of the Rapture given in different portions of the Bible.

The Rapture of Enoch: The story of Enoch is found in the fifth chapter of Genesis. Very little is told of the events of his life, but we can perceive certain significant things about him. Counting Adam as the first generation, Enoch represented the seventh generation to be born into the world. He was the great-grandfather of Noah. We know that he was a righteous man for the Bible states that *"Enoch walked with God"* **(Genesis 5:22).**

"And all the days of Enoch were three hundred sixty and five years: and Enoch walked with God: and he was not; for God took him'" **(Genesis 5:23-24)**

Enoch was not blessed with as many years of life as others of his family line, for he lived upon the world only 365 years. Adam lived to be 930-years old, which Enoch's own son, Methuselah, lived to be 969-years old, an age longer than any other person mentioned in the Bible. Up until Enoch, the fewest number of years any of his family line had lived was 895 years. But Enoch was not cheated, for he was taken out of the world without having to die. His life shows us a type of the "Rapture of the Church."

Enoch was born 622 years after Adam and Eve were driven out of the Garden of Eden.

He was taken from the world 987 years after the Fall. Six-hundred and sixty-nine years later, in the days of Noah, the Flood came upon the world. Here we receive a sign that seems to be directed toward those people living in the world since the particular number system we now employ came into use. When the pages of Genesis were first penned, other figures were used to designate numbers, and the year value given for the time between the "rapture" of Enoch and the Flood might not have carried any special meaning to them at all. The "hidden" meaning which we can see and they could not is, simply, if the third digit of 669 were inverted, we have the number of the Antichrist, 666.

I believe the story of Enoch, included with the story of the Flood, shows us a picture of the Rapture of the Church, the coming to power of the Antichrist during the Tribulation Period, and the gathering of the saved into an "Ark of Safety" while Christ fights the battle of Armageddon. In this illustration, the Rapture of the Church clearly happens before the Tribulation Period.

The Story of Lot: The story of Lot's deliverance from Sodom is short and to the point, but it serves to demonstrate a church typical of many in the last days before the coming of Christ at the Rapture. Lot, though greatly soiled by his association with the sinful inhabitants of Sodom, was nevertheless a child of God. When the angels of the Lord arrived to destroy the wicked city, they were not allowed to do so until Lot and his family were given ample time to leave so they would not be harmed. The nephew of Abraham had compromised his witness to the extant that his sons-in-law did not believe him when he tried to warn them of the impending doom. Only after Lot and his most immediate family had journeyed far from the city did the angels proceed to bring it to destruction. In the same manner, only after the Church has been taken out of the world will the seven years of the Tribulation Period fall upon those who remain behind (a special added note here is that, even though the story of Lot may be used to show certain things about the Rapture of the Church, it is also a very accurate type of the special "rapture" at the close of the Tribulation Period).

Joseph and the Church: Joseph is a well-known personage in the Bible. Most children learn about him at an early age, and, about his coat of many colors. The fact that he experienced dreams, was favored by his father, Jacob, and was consequently hated by his brothers are also familiar facts in his life. He has often been compared with Christ for there are many things in common between their lives. Both were greatly beloved by their father; both were sent to their brethren; both were rejected by their brethren; Joseph was sold for 20 pieces of silver, while Christ was sold for 30 pieces of silver; and both were taken to the land of Egypt, Joseph to serve in slavery, and Jesus to escape the wrath of Herod. But there is also a second symbolism in the trip to Egypt. By Joseph's own words, he was sent before into the land of Egypt to prepare the way for his brethren. In the same sense, when Christ returned to heaven before the Church, he went before us to make preparations for us. *"I go to prepare a place for you"* **(John 14:2)**.

Christ was buried in the tomb of a Joseph, while Joseph was "buried" in the king's prison; both were "resurrected," Joseph to rule with the Pharaoh, and Christ to rule with the Father; both marry Gentile brides; Joseph dispensed bread to a starving world, and Christ spoke of himself as the Bread of Life; both were saviors, Joseph to the known world, and Christ to the world of all ages; Joseph interceded for his brethren, while Christ intercedes for the reborn brethren; during the famine, Joseph's brethren come to him, while, during the Tribulation Period the Jews will come to Christ; Joseph revealed himself to his brethren and was accepted, and, at the return of Christ the nation of Israel will accept him; Joseph established his brethren in Goshen, while Christ will re-establish the modern Jews in their own land.

In several ways, Joseph also has several things in common with the Church. The true followers of the Lord are not looked upon with great favor by the world in general. Just as Christ was persecuted, he warned his apostles that they would also suffer at the hands of the world. In many places in today's world, those who profess Christianity are handled quite roughly, some even being put to death. Many are forbidden to practice their faith by the laws of the land, and are forced to worship as did the Roman Christians, in secret meetings in the catacombs. In America, we are comparatively free from persecution for the time being, but pressure is ever being placed to passed to pass more and more laws to hinder the work of Christ, and to eventually crush the churches and put them out of business completely.

Joseph was thrown into prison under false pretenses; Satan seeks to shackle the work of the Church, using false insinuations to cause the world to turn upon the Lord's movement in the world. Joseph, by the hand of God, was released from prison, just as the Rapture of the Church will set all Christians free. Joseph stood before the pharaoh; the Church will stand before the throne of Christ. Joseph was married soon after this, while the Church, the Bride of Christ, will participate in the Marriage Supper of the Lamb. The Church will experience wonderful years of bliss in the presence of the Lord, while the terrible years of the Tribulation are unfolding on the earth. Joseph was then united with his brethren, just as the Church will be united with the world's brethren when Christ returns at the close of the seven years of great tribulation.

Joseph was twenty-eight years old when he was cast into prison. He remained there for a period of about two years. At the age of thirty, he was released to stand before the Pharaoh. He enjoyed nine years of blissfulness, and was then reunited with his brethren at the age of thirty-nine. As we have already seen, if we stretch the twenty-two years of Josephs life (from his betrayal to his reunion with his brethren), to line up with the Days of Noah (from the Fall of Adam to the Flood of Noah) they are remarkably proportionate to one another. The release of Joseph from prison line up very well with the Rapture of Enoch. This particular comparison does seem to imply that there might be a short while between the Rapture of the Church and the beginning of the seven-year tribulation. Though the traditional time placed between the Rapture and the Return of Christ to the world is usually placed at seven years, I personally know of no place in the Bible where it actually says so. In fact, the comparison between the Days of Noah and the life of Joseph seems to imply that there might be a short while between the Rapture of the Church and the beginning of the seven-year tribulation. It could very likely take the world a limited period of time to reorganize and discover the leadership abilities of the Antichrist—in the wake of so many people suddenly disappearing. But the truth that we should notice here is that, even in the years of Joseph, the "rapture" does seem to precede the years that depict the time of the Tribulation.

At a yet unknown future date, Christ, bringing with him the souls of those that have died in salvation **(I Thessalonians 4:14),** will return to the very vicinity of the earth in order to call the members of the Church out of the world. At this wondrous event, Christ will halt in the air while the souls of the redeemed return to the earth and are first resurrected in their bodies. Then, all of the saved, both living and resurrected, will be caught up together to meet the Lord in the air **(I Thessalonians 4:13-18 & I Corinthians 15:51-53).** The Blessed Hope of the Church will at last be brought forth in reality!

James F. Webb

years of the Tribulation are unfolding on the earth. Joseph was then united with his brethren, just as the Church will be united with the world's brethren when Christ returns at the close of the seven years of great tribulation.

Joseph was twenty-eight years old when he was cast into prison. He remained there for a period of about two years. At the age of thirty, he was released to stand before the Pharaoh. He enjoyed nine years of blissfulness, and was then reunited with his brethren at the age of thirty-nine. As we have already seen, if we stretch the twenty-two years of Josephs life (from his betrayal to his reunion with his brethren), to line up with the Days of Noah (from the Fall of Adam to the Flood of Noah) they are remarkably proportionate to one another. The release of Joseph from prison line up very well with the Rapture of Enoch. This particular comparison does seem to imply that there might be a short while between the Rapture of the Church and the beginning of the seven-year tribulation. Though the traditional time placed between the Rapture and the Return of Christ to the world is usually placed at seven years, I personally know of no place in the Bible where it actually says so. In fact, the comparison between the Days of Noah and the life of Joseph seems to imply that there might be a short while between the Rapture of the Church and the beginning of the seven-year tribulation. It could very likely take the world a limited period of time to reorganize and discover the leadership abilities of the Antichrist—in the wake of so many people suddenly disappearing. But the truth that we should notice here is that, even in the years of Joseph, the "rapture" does seem to precede the years that depict the time of the Tribulation.

At a yet unknown future date, Christ, bringing with him the souls of those that have died in salvation **(I Thessalonians 4:14),** will return to the very vicinity of the earth in order to call the members of the Church out of the world. At this wondrous event, Christ will halt in the air while the souls of the redeemed return to the earth and are first resurrected in their bodies. Then, all of the saved, both living and resurrected, will be caught up together to meet the Lord in the air **(I Thessalonians 4:13-18 & I Corinthians 15:51-53).** The Blessed Hope of the Church will at last be brought forth in reality!

James F. Webb

Chapter 11
The Judgment Seat of Christ and the Marriage of the Lamb

"For we shall all stand before the judgment seat of Christ" **(Romans 14:10b)**

When the Rapture occurs, the Church will accompany Christ away from the world, where they will spend at least seven years enjoying the blessings of heaven while in the actual presence of the Lord. However, before entering that blissful home, Christians will pass through a special examination.

Every person who has ever lived, or shall live upon this world will at some time stand in judgment. This includes the saved as well as the lost. The great difference is the particular judgment we stand in.

Immediately after the Rapture, the Church will stand before the Judgment Seat of Christ, where we will give account of our Christian lives. *"We must all appear before the Judgment Seat of Christ, that every one may receive the things done in the body, according to that he hath done, whether it be good or bad"* **(II Corinthians 5:10).**

A Christian is bought by the precious blood of Jesus Christ, and saved from the condemnation that would send him to hell. He is freed from the Law, having died to it. But he belongs to Christ, and, therefore, must answer to Jesus for the things done in the body after the moment of Salvation. It is believed that the third chapter of I Corinthians speaks of the Judgment Seat of Christ.

"Now if any man build upon this foundation [Jesus Christ] gold, silver, precious stones, wood, hay, stubble; every man's work shall be made manifest: for the day [Day of Judgment] shall declare it, because it shall be revealed by fire; and the fire shall try every man's work of what sort it is. If any man's work abide which he hath built thereupon, he shall receive a reward. If any man's work shall be burned, he shall suffer loss: but he himself shall be saved; yet so as by fire" **(I Corinthians 3:12-15).**

As ore is brought forth from the ground consisting of both precious metal and other worthless elements, the Christian stands before the Judgment Seat of Christ, clothed in good and bad works. He is tried by the flame of the Holy Spirit.

I once spoke to a class of young people concerning the Judgment Seat of Christ, explaining the same verses quoted above, which imply that the Bible seems to tell us will all be tried by fire. I am afraid I shocked some of those present, apparently leaving a few of them with the impression that even Christians would have to go through a hell-like experience in which we would all be, even if only for a short time, engulfed by flames.

But it had not been my intention to imply that all Christians would have to bear the pain of burning before the Judgment Seat of Christ, so I attempted to relieve their fears by reminding them of the story in Daniel of the three Hebrew men who were cast without mercy into the fiery furnace. As the inferno of flames danced about them, they strolled casually about as though they walked by a refreshing stream and enjoyed the blessing of a cool breeze.

In regards to the flame that will try Christians before the seat of Christ, it really should not matter whether we stand in the midst of the inferno, clothed in a body composed of our works, or if we will stand and watch the flames test our works which have been stacked in a great pile. I believe the important thing to remember is that the fire spoken of at that time will not be a flame of punishment, but a method of purification. Even if we ourselves should literally be engulfed within the flame, and witness the tragic sight of many of our works being consumed and vanishing away as smoke and ashes, we can do so in the confidence that we will also be equally encompassed about by the tender love and protection of our Lord and Savior. Though it is true that some will suffer loss of possessions, I suspect that the only pain endured will be the pain of disappointment. I remember the words of the great hymn, "How Firm a Foundation." They say, "The flame shall not hurt thee—I only design thy dross to consume and thy gold to refine."

At the Judgment Seat of Christ, the Christian will give account of his service, and will be purified for all Eternity. He will come before the throne bearing all the deeds of his Christian life; he will leave the throne a precious jewel, a glorified being in every way. He will not be tried for anything in his life that took place before he became a Christian. Those things were all paid for when Jesus shed his blood on the Cross of Calvary. In fact, every sin we commit, whether before or after our salvation, has already been paid for by the sacrifice of Christ.

To properly understand the Judgment Seat of Christ we should first understand the different roles played by God the Father and God the Son. The Father declared that the penalty of sin was death, and death passed upon every man when Adam disobeyed God in the Garden of Eden. Unless a "substitute" could be found, every man would have to pay his own debt when he died, and that debt was more than just physical death. It also involved the soul, which meant hell.

Since all of mankind are the descendants of Adam, all fall under the same curse, because they inherit in their mortal flesh the seed of sin. Sooner or later, in everybody's life, that seed inevitably blossoms out. *"Wherefore, as by one man sin entered into the world, and death by sin; and so death passed upon all men, for all have sinned"* **(Romans 5:12).**

But even before the act of creation began, the substitute was already there and waiting. God the Son, who planned and designed all things in the manner he desired, composed the greatest love story the world shall ever see. He who made us, knowing before that we would fail the test against sin, wrote his own death into the plot that we might have a chance for redemption. *"Greater love hath no man than this, that a man lay down his life for his friends"* **(John 15:13).**

When Jesus lay down his life on Golgotha that April day, he paid off, once and for all, the debt that had fallen upon us even from the time of Adam and Eve. God the Father marked the great debt Paid in Full! and, when a debt is paid, ownership goes to the one who has paid that debt, and that person is the Lord Jesus Christ.

Because Christ bought us with his own sinless blood, we no longer answer to the death sentence, for that is now past. We died to that debt when we died with Christ, through the baptism of the Holy Spirit at the moment of salvation. We are reminded of the Jewish calendar, and the method of using two months bearing the name "Adar." Symbolically, the first Adar represents the first man, Adam. From him we inherit a life that can be nothing else but imperfect, for, as in the calendar, without correction, everything goes wrong as time continues. Therefore, the Second Adar (the second Adam) is intercalated at just the right time, and things are made right. As we are born the physical children of Adam, even so we can, by being born again, become the spiritual children of the Lord.

"Therefore as by the offense of one judgment came upon all men to condemnation; even so by the righteousness of one the free gift came upon all men unto justification of life. For as by one man's disobedience many were made sinners, so by the obedience of one shall many be made righteous" **(Roman 5:18-19).**

The location of this judgment is not known with surety, but will not be upon the earth, for the Church, at that time, shall already have been called forth at the Rapture. It also will not be a judgment to determine a heaven or hell destiny—in fact, it will not deal with salvation at all. It will be a judgment to ascertain Reward for Service.

We have been bought with a price. We have been saved from the original condemnation of sin, but we are not saved from a responsibility to Jesus Christ, who, in order to redeem us, poured out his own life's blood on Calvary's Cross. We must answer to him, whether our acts have been good or bad; whether we have obeyed his commandments or not; whether we have dome the things which the Holy Spirit bade us do. In other words, the Judgment Seat of Christ appraises faithfulness and obedience. Blessed is the man who, when Christ shall appear, *"may have confidence, and not be ashamed before him at his coming"* **(I John 2:28).**

The Bible speaks of five crowns which will be rewarded to Christians for various reasons.

(1) **The Crown of Righteousness:** This crown will be given to all who love his appearing" **(II Timothy 4:7-8).**
(2) **The Incorruptible Crown:** This crown is to be given to the believers who are steadfast in their service. They achieve their reward through faithfulness, their works not

being cast-a-way by the flames of judgment **(I Corinthians 9:25-27)**.
(3) **The Crown of Life:** Primarily related to the Tribulation, although a crown that others have won through the ages, it is awarded to all who are martyred for the cause of Christ **(Revelation 2:10)**.
(4) **The Crown of Rejoicing:** This is the crown awarded to the soul winners. I suspect it also will include those who faithfully witness to others about the grace of God and the way of salvation **(I Thessalonians 2:19-20)**.
(5) **The Crown of Glory:** This is usually considered to be the faithful Pastor's crown. In his mercy and understanding, the Lord may also include those who assume spiritual leadership in various rolls, whether they are ordained ministers or not **(I Peter 5:2-4)**.

The Marriage Supper of the Lamb will follow at this time, a wondrous feats of rejoicing and fellowship. All of the "saved", between the Fall and the Rapture, will be present at this feast. Included among those in attendance will be the "saved" of other dispensations. This was understood by john the Baptist, for he made it clear to those who came to him that he was not the Messiah, but the one to announce him. *"Ye yourselves bear me witness, that I said, I am not the Christ, but that I am sent before him. He that hath the bride is the bridegroom: but the friend of the bridegroom, which standeth and heareth him, rejoiceth greatly because of the bridegroom's voice: this my joy therefore is fulfilled"* **(John 3:28-29)**.

Some believe the wedding supper will not take place until after the Tribulation Period, while some believe it will not happen until the Millennial Kingdom has yielded to the endless years of Eternity. Others are of the opinion that it will have already transpired before Christ returns at the close of the Tribulation Period.

But, in the twenty second chapter of Matthew, Jesus speaking of the Kingdom of Heaven, likens it to a king who prepared a marriage for his son. At the event, a man is discovered who is not wearing a wedding garment.

"And he [the king] *saith unto him, Friend, how camest thou in hither not having a wedding garment" And he was speechless. then said the king to the servants, Bind him hand and foot, and take him away, and cast him into outer darkness; there shall be weeping and gnashing of teeth. for many are called, but few are chosen"* **(Matthew 22:12-14).**

These verses remind me of verses in the book of Revelation, where it speaks of war in heaven.

"And there was war in heaven: Michael and his angels fought against the dragon; and the dragon fought and his angels, and prevailed not; neither was their place found any more in heaven. And the great dragon was cast out, that old serpent, called the Devil, and Satan, which deceiveth the whole world: he was cast out into the earth, and his angels were cast out with him" **(Revelation 12:7-9).**

The quote from Matthew, if it does speak of the same incident as found in Revelation 12, seems to condense into one continuous happening the entire story of the matter of Satan, which is told in two separate happenings in the last book of the Bible. The Devil, fighting to prevent his ousting from heaven and failing in that endeavor, comes to earth with a vengeance. He takes control of the antichrist and leases his terrible persecution of Jewish people, but is stopped, once and for all, with the return of the Lord. At that point, the rest of the event, which is described in Matthew, comes to pass. An angel binds Satan and casts him into the bottomless pit, where he will remain for one-thousand years. See **Revelation 20:1-3.**

Although we think of a pit as a hole dug into the earth, the earth does have a theoretical center beyond which an object, cast into a pit leading to that spot, would seem to reach a point where it would fall no more, therefore finding a spot constituting a center. But space seems to have no end, and very well might be considered bottomless. This could be what Matthew refers to as *"outer darkness."*

When Christ comes in the air at the Rapture, and calls forth his Church from the world, the individual members of the Church will pass through a judgment of works. Then, there will follow a time of great rejoicing as those who believed and trusted in their Lord, with all the shackles of sin and shame now placed forever in the past, finally meet in full fellowship the very one who loved and saved them. The Church is the promised bride of Christ, and has been espoused for over nineteen-hundred years. The formal binding of Christ with the Church surely will not be put off until another distant point in history, but will happen at that time.

The Bible is very explicit in certain things. *"I will come again, and receive you unto myself; that where I am, there will ye be also"* **(John 14:3b).** *"Then we which are alive and remain shall be caught up together with them* [the resurrected saints] *in the clouds, to meet the Lord in the air; and so shall we ever be with the Lord"* *(***I Thessalonians 4:17).**

These verses, without doubt, speak of the Rapture, and they are dogmatic in one special thought. The Church, after being rescued from the world by the Rapture, will never be separated from Christ again! This is not true of one who is only espoused to another. In Jewish law, for the full period of espousal, the couple may not be with one another save in the company of one who has been appointed to chaperon them. They are permitted to dismiss the services of the chaperon at the wedding supper, when they are joined in marriage.

The Church is pictured in the Old Testament in the story of Isaac's bride. Abraham directed his most faithful servant to go to the land of his brethren and find a bride for his son, Isaac. The servant was faithful in that quest, following the leadership of the Lord, and selected Rebekah. She willingly accompanied the servant back to the land of her husband-to-be. In this story, we see the Holy spirit working with the future bride of the Son of God. Just as the faithful servant sought out Rebekah and asked her to be the bride of Isaac, so even does the Holy Spirit seek out candidates for the Church, and asks them to become members of the bride of Christ. Then, just as the servant accompanied the soon-to-be bride of Isaac throughout the journey to her future home, even so does the Holy Spirit dwell with the Church on the journey through life, delivering the espoused bride safe to the groom at the appointed time.

"Let us be glad and rejoice, and give honour to him: for the marriage of the Lamb is come, and his wife hath made herself ready. And to her was granted that she should be arrayed in fine linen, clean

and white: for the fine linen is the righteousness of saints" **(Revelation 19:7-8).**

These things take place before the Lord returns to the earth at the close of the seven years of tribulation, for the following verses speak of the Lord coming to the earth as King of Kings, and Lord of Lords, and riding upon a white horse, with many hosts of heaven in his train that they appear as the clouds of heaven.

But, before the return to the earth with Christ, there will be many things to see and learn in the heavenly setting we will find ourselves in, so the years will not be idle. It will be a time of "true" education, before the Church returns with the Lord during the one-thousand years of the earthly kingdom.

It will also be a time which will witness the renewal of many past acquaintances. The greatest reunion in the history of time will unfold, as loved ones and friends will meet again with the knowledge that there will be no more parting of the ways, or no more sad farewells. And the best realization of all will be the fact that we will be able to fellowship, face to face, with the Lord Jesus Christ, and to know him on a personal basis never before possible!

"Now we see through a glass, darkly; but then face to face: now I know in part; but then shall I know even as also I am known" **(1 Corinthians 13:12).**

While the storm of tribulation is progressing on the earth, those invited to the Marriage Supper of the Lamb will truly be experiencing "heavenly" things while far above the strife and the agony below.

"Praise ye the Lord. Sing unto the Lord a new song, and his praise in the congregation of saints" **(Psalm 149:1).**

Chapter 12
The Coming of Antichrist and Tribulation

"And I stood on the sand of the sea, and saw a beast rise up out of the sea, having seven heads and ten horns, and upon his horns ten crowns, and upon his heads the name of blasphemy" **(Revelation 13:1).**

A man is going to appear on the scene whom the world will deem a superman. He is spoken of in the Bible. In the eyes of the world, he will seem to have the answers to all of the problems of civilization, and he will ride to power on tidings of peace and prosperity. In truth, he will deceive many, but most of the world will follow after him as though he were a messiah.

He is referred to in the book of Revelation as the first beast, and, elsewhere in the Bible as the Antichrist. His actual reign upon the earth will be one of such death and destruction that Christ referred to it as the time of *"great tribulation, such as was not since the beginning of the world"* (**Matthew 24:21).**

I do not know if the seven-year period of tribulation follows immediately after the Rapture of the Church or not. From my own observations, I would say that most of those who teach about the "last days" do lean in that direction. That would seem to mean that the person whom the Bible calls the Antichrist will already be very much on the scene when the Church is taken out of the world. But, his complete rise to the position of power pictured in the Bible may require a duration of one to two years. This would not really be contradictory to Bible prophecy. It would only mean that Daniel's seventieth week would simply begin a little later than some have interpreted.

The real Antichrist will probably not be recognized by the Church before the Rapture occurs. We may have suspicions, but that is happening even today as people, who are familiar with the prophecies of the coming world dictator, try to select a candidate for that position from contemporary public figures. But his rise to power will be deceptive, for he will appear before the world as a man of peace (the rider on the white horse of **Revelation 6:2**). He will please many with his ability to make decisions which seem to benefit all nations, and multitudes will favor him.

But what of the aftereffects of the Rapture upon the world? Will there suddenly be great voids in the population, and much confusion and disarray in governments and services to the common people? Some teach that the world will be sent a strong delusion so they will not realize that large masses of people are even missing. But such a delusion would not cover certain very precise circumstances, such as: a doctor suddenly disappearing while in the midst of an operation; a paper route not being delivered; the pilot of an airplane vanishing; or the driver of a bus, or car, or so forth.

Surely the absence of so many people will be noticed in one way or another, and its effect upon the world might be far greater than some suspect, depending, of course, on the percentage of Christians making up the population in different locations, towns, and countries throughout the earth. Some places may actually find themselves without the main core of their governments, or their law enforcement agencies sadly low in strength, while, others may notice little difference at all.

Whether or not some may realize what has happened, at least certain portions of the world may find themselves in a state of catastrophe and confusion. There could be situations where strong and extreme action may be necessary to reinstate order and some stability. A military rule would probably take over in such a case, of course assuring the citizens of that country that it would be only temporary, lasting long enough until elections could be organized.

Such a scenario would place one man in a seat of great authority, especially if he had the armed forces of his country behind him. The populace would follow, also, if he had a soothing personality, and calmed the citizens with actions and brought conditions back to a degree of normalcy.

I do not know that the Antichrist will arise to power in this fashion, but it is a possibility. It is also possible that he is simply elected to public office by the people, or, that he is already the leader of a country when the Rapture occurs. But, if he is not already in power, he will certainly become a world power shortly after the Church has been caught away. The world will not realize that along with the "favored" dictator will also come the Great Tribulation.

The Tribulation Period will not break suddenly upon the world without warning. Storm clouds have been gathering for a very long time, and are even now on the horizon, if honest people will only open their eyes to the truth. Early forecasts were issued by the Bible many centuries ago. General prophecies, partially fulfilled in all ages, make up a portion of the long list, but very numerous predictions, too precise to be mistaken, are also present.

Christ refers to several warning events in the twenty-fourth chapter of Matthew. He mentions wars and rumors of wars, tension among nations, famines, pestilences, and earthquakes. It is an undisputable fact that the present age does qualify on all counts.

The last few decades have witnessed a distressing thing in the religious world. Conservatism and Fundamentalism in Bible theology have undergone a steady decline. There have been revivals, but modern philosophy seems to find delight in denying the true things of God. Astrology, witchcraft, seances, dabbling with familiar spirits, and Satan worship have made inroads into the mainstream of society. Even many church groups have suffered in their basic doctrines due to these influences. It is an age of turning away from the paths of truth, and following after itching ears.

"For the time will come when they will not endure sound doctrine; but after their own lusts shall heap to themselves teachers, having itching ears; and they shall turn away their ears from the truth, and shall be turned unto fables" **(II Timothy 4:3-4).** The book of Thessalonians says that *"that day* [the day of Christ] *shall not come, except there come a falling away first."* This falling away from the things of God is known as the Apostasy.

Today, it is popular to speak of one-world things, one mind concerning the way men should govern themselves, one philosophy concerning life and the manner in which children should be raised, and one way in which life came into existence. The ecumenical movement encourages closer ties between the differing factions of Christianity and a watered-down version of what constitutes right and wrong, while the nations of the world move toward a single authoritative government.

But these human efforts are doomed to failure because the imperfect nature and flesh of men keeps getting in the way. In the case of religion, there can never be a successful union of different doctrines unless each denomination gives up something which it believes in order to enter into equal brotherhood with a denomination teaching a different doctrine. If any denomination can do this, it is an absolute indication that the members of that church could not have had a very deep faith in their own creed to start with.

While the Church is clothed in mortal flesh, no one-world religion will fully take control. The union shall come, but only through the Holy Spirit when the members of the Church receive their glorified bodies, after the Rapture. However, in the world, such a unified religion will occur for a while, under the guidance of the Antichrist, and his False Prophet.

But from the time of Adam and Eve, if history and the study of dispensations prove anything, it is that human beings, if given enough time and leeway, will usually mess things up. It would almost seem that man, without God in his life, cannot rule himself effectively. A truly one-world government will come, but only after the Return of Christ, and Christ himself will be the ruler.

But the world keeps trying. With countless national, world, and economic problems accelerating at an all-time rate, the ever growing population of earth has sought exhaustively for a workable solution. Tiring of trouble and almost insurmountable dilemma, the world is anxiously looking for a veritable superman who can solve the very perplexing conditions of the age, and bring the clashing factions of modern civilization into harmony.

The trend is evident in politics, as the age hurries after candidates with attractive personalities and rainbow answers to society's ills. It does not seem to matter if the remedy really works in the long run, as long as the doctor prescribes the medicine the people desire. Such a man is almost worshipped by the multitude. It is an age leaning toward living idols.

In their irrational attempt to ignore the one true God, men have sought to find solutions within their own ranks. Therefore, mankind will become assenting victims to the tempting illusion of the Antichrist when he comes upon the scene.

"I am come in my Father's name, and ye receive me not: if another shall come in his own name, him ye will receive" **(John 5:43)**.

One of the greatest and most specific signs given in the Bible concerning the Last Days is the Rebirth of Israel as a nation.

"For I am with thee, saith the Lord, to save thee: though I make a full end of all nations whither I have scattered thee, yet will I not make a full end of thee" **(Jeremiah 30:11)**.

"And I will bring again the captivity of my people of Israel, and they shall build the waste cities...and they shall no more be pulled up out of their land which I have given them, saith the Lord thy God" **(Amos 9:14-15)**.

There are many Bible verses which refer to this rebirth, among which are: **Isaiah 11:11; Jeremiah 16:14-15; Jeremiah 31:35-36;** and the thirty-seventh chapter of **Ezekiel.**

In **Ezekiel 37,** the dispersed nation of Israel is compared to a valley of dry bones. The prophet watches as God calls the seemingly dead bones back together again, covering them with sinew and flesh, and resurrecting a large multitude of people. The chapter refers to the national restoration of Israel. It is also clear that the Rebirth of Israel includes all twelve tribes, as shown by the two sticks joined into one.

Christ, of course, speaks of the restoration of the Jews to their land when he refers to the budding of the fig tree in **Matthew 24:32-34.** But, although Israel was reborn in A.D. 1948, as prophesied, they returned in unbelief as far as recognizing the true Messiah, Jesus of Nazareth. Therefore, peace has eluded that land, and they have lived under the constant threat of countries about them. How can they experience true peace unless they have known the Prince of Peace?

"O Jerusalem, Jerusalem, thou that killest the prophets, and stonest them which are sent unto thee, how often would I have gathered thy children together, even as a hen gathereth her chickens under her wings, and ye would not! Behold, your house is left unto you desolate. For I say unto you, Ye shall not see me henceforth, till

ye shall say, Blessed is he that cometh in the name of the Lord" **(Matthew 23:37-39).**

Because peace has so persistently eluded the Middle East, the attention of the world has been dramatically focused on this small region. In spite of the rather insignificant size of so many of its countries, events happening in this area have severely affected the rest of the planet.

Bible scholars are not entirely united when they try to place in chronology of the last days the events describes in the thirty-eighth and thirty-ninth chapters of Ezekiel. These two chapters are generally recognized as foretelling an invasion of Israel by its powerful and large northern neighbor, Russia. Some teach that these things will transpire before the Rapture occurs; others teach that they will happen in the first part of the seven years of tribulation, some even trying to coincide it with the Battle of Armageddon.

I believe that the invasion by Russia will be a completely separate occurrence from Armageddon. And, if it should unfold near the Rapture or the first portion of the Tribulation Period, it would greatly simplify the Mid-East situation, and path the way for the entrance of the Antichrist.

So, a man is going to appear on the scene whom the world will deem a superman. Apparently he will rise to power without opposition, the world desiring his leadership in the belief that he possesses the unequaled ability to direct the world out of its misery.

Whatever his racial background may actually be, he will ascend to power in a Gentile nation. His authority will be greatly amplified by an alliance of several nations, generally referred to collectively as the Revived Roman Empire (the Empire of Rome was actually comprised of ten nations). Many see significant signs of this "revival" in NATO, and, in the growth of the European Common Market. The United States of America is already a member of NATO, and has ever sought a closer relationship with the potential giant of the European Market. At present, the strongest member of the European alliance is Germany. This would seem to be a very meaningful fact when it is remembered that for centuries, after the fall of the original Roman empire, it was Germany that bore the title of the "Holy Roman empire."

World problems, together with the plight of energy and economic crisis, has hastened the binding of these nations together. The nations of Europe, standing alone, have found themselves too small and insignificant to make the world as a whole pay very much attention to their problems. But, as a unified force, the other nations of earth will be required to listen to them.

It is not certain just how much the Antichrist literally has to do with the forming of the United States of Europe, but it does seem apparent that he secures a close tie with the organization, and soon rises to the position of its head.

The Bible does not seem to assert that the nations comprising this alliance are ever to be molded together as solidly as are the United States of America. The European states are the ten toes of Nebuchadnezzar's image, made of iron intermingled with clay. The relationship will be brittle, never reaching a point where their collective condition may be termed "one nation." The union will be one of convenience, to present a power block in the face of opposition.

The First Beast (the Antichrist) may originate in one of the countries within this alliance **(Revelation 13:1).** However, it does not necessarily follow that he will initially rise to power in the same country of his birth. The world is full of political opportunities, and there are many nations which would offer a position of power to a man who seemed able to deliver the goods.

It should also be remembered that the final rise to power by the antichrist will take place after the Rapture of the Church. At that time, even a previously Christian nation would then be godless, and, therefore, a possible candidate for the kingdom of the beast if it possessed enough arms and military might to impose its will on the rest of the world.

Bible theologians have also pointed out that the ten toes of Nebuchadnezzar's image, which represent the Revived Roman Empire, are located on two separate feet joined to the legs of the body. So, it is conceivable that the actual empire may be located in two separate localities with a division between them, either of land, or of water, or an ocean.

It does not appear that the Antichrist ever succeeds in fully establishing a literal one-world government. The Bible tells us that all the world wonders after him in admiration, and at one point even joins in worshiping him. However, it should be pointed out that the tern, "all the world", used in **Revelation 13:3,** is shown to be a general figure of speech, when we consider the rest of the book of Revelation. Not every single person in the world will follow the Antichrist, for the Bible tells us that there will be many people slain during the reign of the beast, because they will not submit to him. There will also be many of the "saved" who will be alive when Christ returns at the close of the seven years, for, the angels will gather them from every part of the earth before the Battle of Armageddon begins.

However, the Antichrist will rule a world of nations brought together by their common hatred of God. With the destruction of Russia's military might upon the mountains of Israel, the kingdom of the beast, allied with the nations of Europe (Revived Roman Empire), is too powerful to be opposed by another earthly force **(Revelation 13:4).**

The Antichrist will be a very popular figure—a hero—when he arrives in the eyes of the world. This is why the sixth chapter of Revelation pictures him as coming upon a white horse. He carries a bow, but there is no mention of arrows, thus implying that he comes in peace **(Daniel 11:21).** However, his reign will be far from a peaceful one. The three horsemen, which follow him in **Revelation 6,** represent war, famine, and death.

To the Jew, the Antichrist will present himself as the long awaited Messiah. Because he apparently comes with answers which seem to solve Israel's problems with unfriendly neighbors, he may be accepted by some of that nation's people.

A covenant will be established between the Antichrist and the nation of Israel, apparently bringing with it the assurance of peace in the Middle East. The covenant will be planned for a period of seven years **(Daniel 9:27)**, and, is usually divided into a first half and a second half by students of the Bible. The seven-year period will probably begin immediately, or at a time not long after the Rapture of the Church (other studies in this book imply that it should be a period no longer than two years). The seven years are commonly referred to as the Tribulation Period, and, sometimes, as the *"time of Jacob's trouble"* **(Jeremiah 30:7)**. They are also believed to be the final week of Daniel's seventy weeks.

Some of the special facts and personal traits of the first beast of **Revelation 13** (the Antichrist) are listed as follows, keeping in mind that, during differing portions of the Tribulation Period, his apparent character will be viewed differently by much of the world.

1. He is considered to be the "little horn" of **Daniel 8**.
2. He will be a vile person [whether or not this trait is recognized at first is not certain] **(Daniel 11:21)**.
3. He will obtain the kingdom by flatteries **(Daniel 11:21)**.
4. He will have power, a throne, and authority.
5. Though his government will be subdivided between ten kings, he will be supreme.
6. He will be a political world dictator.
7. He will not regard the god of his fathers, nor any god **(Daniel 11:37)**.
8. He will magnify himself and honor the god of forces **(Daniel 11:37-38)**.
9. He will not regard the desire of women [some interpret this to imply that the Antichrist will be homosexual, while some interpret the words to mean he will not "honor" the "rights" of women **(Daniel 11:37)**.
10. He will have power over tribes, tongues, and nations.
11. In **Revelation 13**, he is referred to by the Greek word "therion" (translated "beast'), which means a wild, untamed animal. Particularly in the second half of the Tribulation Period, he will appear to be a monster, ruling in terror.
12. His reign will last approximately seven years (concerning Israel), with forty-two months of terror during the last three and one-half years.
13. He will be the world's master blasphemer. Of all those who have been before him, none will equal him, or be able

to touch the hem of his garment in blasphemy: *"and upon his heads the name of blasphemy"* **(Revelation 13:1)**.
14. He will make a seven-year covenant with Israel, assuring peace **(Daniel 9:27)**.
15. In the midst of the seven years, he will turn on Israel and seek to destroy it's people.
16. He will sit up the "abomination that maketh desolation," spoken of by Christ in **Matthew 24:15**, and in **Daniel 9:27; 11:31; and 12:11)**.
17. He will establish strict laws concerning commerce. No one will be able to buy or sell unless they receive a mark in their right hand, or in their forehead. The mark will be given in three ways: a mark, or emblem of some sort; the name of the beast; or the "number" of that name. In some languages, words do have a number value. It is my understanding that the Hebrew and Greek languages do not have special characters to designate numbers. Each letter of their alphabets has a numeric value associated with it. Therefore, any word or name may also be said to have a number value. For instance, the Greek form of "Jesus" adds up to 888. The "number" of the name of the Antichrist is 666 **(Revelation 13:18)**. It should also be noted here that there is a reasonable theory that the "mark" might, in some way, include a computer chip holding special data concerning the individual.
18. He will set up a "living" image of himself in the temple, and will compel the Jewish people to worship it, and will execute those who will not **(Revelation 13:14-15)**. Several years ago, I visited a trade show in Tulsa where many large companies set up booths and exhibits. One display especially stood out to me. The central source of voice contact with those who viewed the exhibit was provided by a simple mannequin type head, bearing no features at all, and white in color. A hidden camera projected upon the head the likeness of a man speaking words. I was impressed how very realistic the image seemed to be. If

such feats were accomplished several years ago, what type of "image" could be produced by the wonders of the modern age. I suspect that the image, spoken of in the Book of Revelation, will be quite capable of carrying on a conversation with those who come before it.

The largest portion of the **Book of Revelation** deals with the Tribulation Period. Bible authorities do differ somewhat in their individual interpretations of the chronological order of events, some insisting that all happenings unfold in the exact order as given in the text, while others maintain there are divisions in the book which, in dealing with particular topics, go beyond the boundary of strict chronological order. After the single topic is exhausted, the reader is often returned to an earlier date, and, another topic is pursued.

It is obvious that not every detail is supplied concerning the Tribulation Period. But this is not necessary, since God has provided enough information to allow even the most apathetic of believers to recognize the scene as it unfolds upon the earth—and the scene will not be a pleasant one. Destruction and trial beyond the imagination will fall upon this planet during that short span of time. The abandonment of morality will combine with the unleashed forces of nature to plunge humanity toward the very brink of extermination. But even amid the toppling ruins of man's civilization, God will yet perform a good work.

There will be people "saved" after the Rapture and during the Tribulation Period, but they will not be members of the Church. That title is reserved only for those who are born again between the Cross and the catching away of the Church from earth. But this fact does not mean that "salvation" is any less real to those of the Tribulation, nor that God loves them less. The saved of the Tribulation Period will endure severe and trying hardships and persecution, with large numbers being forced to suffer actual martyrdom. These people, dying for their Lord, will be both Jew and Gentile **(Revelation 6:9-11; and 7:9-14).**

A very select group of people will be picked and set aside for special service. They will be chosen from the twelve tribes of Israel, and, therefore, will be of the Jewish race. Their number will be 144-thousand (12,000 from each tribe). Though opinions differ concerning the mission of these people, many believe they will be preachers proclaiming the free gift of the Lord's Redemption, and the proximity of the Kingdom. The group will be sealed in their foreheads with *"the seal of the living God,"* apparently to shield them until their mission is completed.

Some teach that these especially chosen Jewish people will eventually be martyred, but others believe they will be preserved throughout the darkened days of the Tribulation Period, though, perhaps, they will be unable to work openly for the last portion of that time.

There will be two Babylons prominent in the world during the last days. One will be a political empire; the other will be a religious organization. It is theorized that the Antichrist will, at some physical point in the seven-year period, locate his government in the physical Babylon.

Ancient Babylon was located on the Euphrates River about 50 miles from Baghdad. It has recently made the news again as the war has raged in modern Iraq. For reasons of tourism, many of its important buildings have been rebuilt, with the intention of eventually restoring the entire city.

References to the Antichrist coming forth from Assyria, or one of the Arabian countries lying in that area of the world, may be true, but there are other possibilities. In the second century before Christ, Antiochus Epiphanes, usually considered to be a type of the future Antichrist, ruled over the area of Assyria. He carried out a great persecution of the Jewish people, and, because many prophecies seemed to be fulfilled in him, it has been thought that the coming Antichrist will also be a native of that part of the world.

Some say that the Babylon of Revelation is symbolic in nature, and that the Antichrist will actually arise in another country bearing many of the characteristics of ancient Babylon. Many believe that the United States of America is fully qualified to be his capital, that the United Nations building is the antitype of the tower of Babel, and that America will align itself with the European Alliance. We must remember that anything is possible, keeping in mind that these things will happen after the Rapture, when all nations on the face of the earth will be godless.

It is also possible that the Antichrist will be born away from the Middle-East. that he will rise to great heights in a Gentile nation, then, as his power begins to assert itself toward one-worldlism, choose to move or establish his capital in the fabulously rebuilt city of Babylon. There are many possibilities, and most beyond the scope of speculation at the present time, but the alert child of God, in those days of tumultuous chaos, should be able to recognize the truth as it unfolds.

Through the first half of the seven-year period, in order to help tie together his empire of allied nations, the Antichrist will use Religious Babylon, because of the great sway that system can exert over the minds of those within its reach. Many believe that this apostate organization will center itself in the city of Rome, mainly because of the bible's words associating it with a city built upon seven hills. Rome is situated on seven hills, so, that city, long held as a religious center by the world, could be the center of the religion advocated by the first beast. However, in all fairness to Rome, once more we must remember that these things happen after the Rapture.

With the true children of God removed from the world, the remaining skeleton of any religious denomination on earth would qualify as the last form of apostate Christendom, the Harlot Church.

A Christian religious organization, without Christ, is a false religion, and soon becomes submerged in debauched worship, idolatry, mistaken practices, and deceptive devotion. It may use the name of the one true God, but worship a god of its own making. It sets up systems, rites, and rituals to replace what God has commanded, but the Bible calls this whoredom, adultery, and fornication **(Jeremiah 3:6, 8-9; Ezekiel 16:32; Hosea 1 & 2; and Revelation 2:22).** This is the spiritual nature of Mystery Babylon **(Revelation 17:5),** and derives its name from the religious system embraced by ancient Babylon.

Somewhere near the center of the Tribulation Period, the Antichrist will desire to further tighten his strong dominance and influence, and encompass what is left of the nations of the world not already fully under his rule. The kings of the alliance will hate the Harlot Church, because, in its present form, it will hinder their progress in reaching the number of remaining nations of the world. The result of this frustration will be that the empire of the Antichrist will turn upon Religious Babylon and destroy it.

Several important events unfold near the center of the seven years of tribulation. One of these takes place in the heavens away from earth.

"And there was war in heaven: Michael and his angels fought against the dragon: and the dragon fought and his angels, and prevailed not; neither was their place found any more in heaven. And the great dragon was cast out, that old serpent, called the Devil, and Satan, which deceiveth the whole world: he was cast out into the earth, and his angels were cast out with him" **(Revelation 12:7-9).**

The verses just quoted from the book of Revelation should not be confused with the occurrence spoken of by Christ in **Luke 10:18.** There, the Lord refers to Satan's initial rebellion against God, before the Garden of Eden. Here, the similar happening transpires during the Tribulation Period.

Lucifer was defeated in his early attempt to overthrow God **(Isaiah 14:12-15),** but has not been prohibited from going to and fro from the heavens, even appearing before the very throne of God where he accuses the saints **(Revelation 11:10; Job 1:12-15).** He has continued to oppose the work of the Lord since Adam and Eve were driven forth from the garden. But here, mid-way in the Tribulation Period, the Devil and his angels are driven forth from heaven once and for all. He comes down to the earth having great wrath, because he knows that he has but a short time **(Revelation 12:12).** It is at this point that Satan, who has already greatly influenced the Antichrist, will completely take him over, and, through him, begin his terrible work against the Jewish people.

Perhaps in retaliation for the destruction of the Harlot Church, or for one of many reasons, an assassination attempt will be made upon the life of Antichrist. The attack will appear to succeed, for his head will suffer a mortal wound, but a new personage will arrive on the scene just in time to change the situation. While the Bible does not actually state that the Antichrist is healed by the Second Beast of **Revelation 13,** most Bible students feel that this is strongly implied. The world will greatly impressed by the miraculous healing of the wound, and the recovery of the powerful dictator. through the work of the Second Beast, the nations of earth will be so awe stricken that they will be led to worship the dragon which gives power to the Antichrist. They will willingly reverence him, commenting, *"Who is like unto the beast? Who is able to able to make war with him"* **(Revelation 13:4)**? Of course, the actual name used in this Biblical quotation may not be used publicly, at least not to the Antichrist directly.

The Antichrist will be a world political figure—a great dictator. The Second Beast of **Revelation 13** will be a religious leader. He is referred to elsewhere in Revelation as the False Prophet. His religious nature is symbolized by his lamb-like appearance **(Revelation 13:11),** but the same verse makes it clear that he will speak as a dragon. He is a definite example of the wolf in sheep's clothing. He is the third person of the Satanic Trinity demonstrated before the world in the last days.

As God and man are both trinities, so Satan chooses to work as a trinity during the Tribulation Period. Parallels existing between the three trinities are given in **Chart 11.**

CHART 11
THE THREE TRINITIES (GOD, MAN, & SATAN)

GOD	MAN	SATAN
(Three in One)	(Three in One)	(Three Separates Working as One)
Father	Soul	Satan
Son	Body	Antichrist
Holy Spirit	Spirit	False Prophet

The trinities involving God, Man, and Satan (during the Tribulation) are demonstrated in this figure. In contrast to the trinities of God and Man, the trinity of Satan is composed of three separate individuals: the Devil himself, and two human beings.

When the Hebrews followed Moses out of the land of Egypt, they worshipped God and carried out certain ordinances by use of the Tabernacle, a tent-like, mobile structure built exactly according to the specifications of God (book of Exodus). Solomon was permitted to construct a more permanent center of worship, the Temple, completed in B.C. 1005.

Through the centuries, the beautiful building suffered greatly at the hands of Israel's enemies. It was destroyed by Babylon in 587 B.C. and, in time, another less elaborate building was raised in the place of the one built by Solomon. Herod the Great erected the one actually in use when Jesus was born. Finally, in A.D. 70, the forces of Rome destroyed this building, also, and no temple has existed until this day. The "Wailing Wall," located in the Old city of Jerusalem, is believed to be the only standing portion of the original Temple (today, the wall is actually thought to be a retaining wall built to hold the earth in place beneath the actual Temple). However, because certain events must transpire during the Tribulation Period, it is suspected that there is a strong possibility that the Jewish Temple will be rebuilt. There are many rumors now existing which say that plans and stones are already being prepared for the building, and, when the right time arrives, the Temple can be raised in a very short while.

"When ye therefore shall see the abomination of desolation, spoken of by Daniel the prophet, stand in the holy place, (whoso readeth, let him understand:) then let them which be in Judea flee into the mountains: let him which is on the housetop not come down to take any thing out of his house: neither let him which is in the field return back to take his clothes. And woe unto them that are with child, and to them that give suck in those days! But pray ye that your flight be not in winter, neither on the sabbath day: for then shall be great tribulation, such as was not since the beginning of the world to this time, no, nor ever shall be" **(Matthew 24:15-21).**

The "Abomination of Desolation" is referred to in the book of **Daniel,** chapter nine.

"And he shall confirm the covenant with many for one week: and in the midst of the week he shall cause the sacrifice and the oblation to cease, and for the overspreading of abominations he shall make it

desolate, even until the consummation, and that determined shall be poured upon the desolate" **(Daniel 9:27).**

Many believe that these verses speak of an act committed by the Antichrist, and that act will be performed in the rebuilt Temple. History relates that Antiochus Epiphanes, the oppressor of the Jews in the second century before Christ, was the prototype of the man of sin, and, Antiochus carried out an abominable act against the Temple in Jerusalem. On December 25, B.C. 168, he offered a sow upon the altar, and erected an altar to Jupiter.

The Antichrist of the last days will also perform an act similar to this. He will be able to accomplish the deed by reason of the armed forces at his disposal. The Bible relates that the sanctuary of strength will be polluted, the daily sacrifice taken away, and the *"abomination that maketh desolate"* shall be placed **(Daniel 11:3).** To those who reason that the prophecy concerning the Abomination of Desolation had its complete fulfillment at the time of Antiochus Epiphanes, and does not apply to a future time, I can only remind them that Jesus Christ warned the Jewish people that the prophecy was also intended for a future date. The verses were quoted above, and are found in **Matthew 24:15-21.**

These references to the Temple ordinances seem to imply that the act will be carried out in the temple itself. The time of execution is foretold by **Daniel 12:11-12,** and appears to be the middle part of the Tribulation Period. The actual nature of the act is not known for certain, but one theory seems to stand out before others.

"And [he] deceiveth them that dwell on the earth by the means of those miracles which he [the false prophet] had power to do in the sight of the beast; saying to them that dwell on the earth, that they should make an image of the beast, that the image of the beast should both speak, and cause that as many as would not worship the beast should be killed" **(Revelation 13:14-15).**

Nebuchadnezzar made a great image and placed it in the plain of Dura, in the province of Babylon **(Daniel 3:1).** Apparently, the king's dream of the preceding chapter. and Daniel's interpretation of that dream, inspired the Babylonian to construct the huge image which he attempted to turn into an idol. We can only assume that he caused the huge statue to be fashioned after his own, since Daniel had pointed out to him that the golden head of the dream's image represented him [Nebuchadnezzar]. the rest of the body was probably made to flatter the king, regardless of his real physique.

The dream had not been given to glorify the king of Babylon, but to show the history of kingdoms to follow, but pride caused Nebuchadnezzar to think more highly of himself than he should. A good ruler should provide wise guidance for his country; he should establish laws for the common welfare of the citizens; but he should never forget that he is only one of those citizens. Above all, he should never seek to establish himself on a level with the one true God. Nebuchadnezzar not only built his image to magnify himself, he went so far as to compel his people to fall down and worship it, and imposed a penalty of death for violators.

The image of the Antichrist will be the antitype of the image erected by the Babylonian king. Its exact measurements, or the manner of its construction, or how it will perform and accomplish the things spoken of in **Revelation 13,** remain a mystery. But it does appear that the "image" of the Antichrist, providing the Jewish temple has been reconstructed by that time, will be placed in that location, and that image will be the fulfillment of the prophecy of the Abomination of Desolation.

Placed in that special location and given the ability of speech, it perhaps will possess the power, by the wonder of modern computer wisdom and the influence of Satan, to literally carry on conversations with those addressing it. All will be required to worship the image, or be killed. It is for this reason that the Lord Jesus Christ, in the twenty-fourth chapter of the Gospel of Matthew, strongly urges all those who dwell in Judea to literally flee for their lives. Many will die at this time, but the most devastating thing about this wretched drama is the fact that many of those unfortunate persons, dying because they refuse to worship the Antichrist, will still perish without recognizing the Lord Jesus as the Messiah and Savior.

It is from this point—when people see *"the abomination of desolation, spoken of by Daniel the prophet, stand in the holy place"*—that the number of days given in **Daniel 12:11** are to be counted.

"And from the time when the daily sacrifice shall be taken away, and the abomination that maketh desolate set up, there shall be a thousand two hundred and ninety days" **(Daniel 12:11.**

Many Bible students believe there will be a point in time when the Return of Christ will be revealed. But only those who are familiar with the book of Daniel will realize this.

Prophecy has been largely forgotten in our day and time, even in some of the Christian churches, in favor of a more socially aligned doctrine. It is now considered stylish to advocate and promote the Church's involvement in matters of physical lifestyle, rather than show concern for a person's spiritual nature. In the general eye of the world, churches should primarily focus the bulk of their work on feeding the hungry, caring for the homeless, and being active in divers crusades against bigotry, helping the poor and downtrodden, orphaned children, and any other cause that helps better the physical state of human beings.

While these things are good projects, and Christians should not turn a deaf ear to the situations abounding in the world, the primary mission of the Church is, and always has been, to tell the world what the Lord has written in his Book; to proclaim to every living person the truth concerning his wonderful gift to mankind; to shout that God himself has provided the remedy for sin which can wash away man's separation from the Creator, through the death of Christ on Calvary's Cross. The main work of the Church is to save souls!

When the Abomination that maketh Desolate unfolds, and the time period of 1,290 days goes into effect, the Church will no longer dwell in the world, so the prophecy of Daniel does not really concern the Church directly. But the knowledge which the Church possesses if of great value to those who must face the cruel years of the Tribulation, and the Jewish souls in the area of Jerusalem may need it in the day foretold by Daniel. The day of the Abomination also marks the beginning of the second Times of the Gentiles, when the Holy City once more will be trodden under foot by Gentile power **(Revelation 11:2).** this three and one-half year span of time should not be confused with the much longer era, referred to as the Times of the Gentiles, which has already ended in A.D. 1967.

"And he causeth all, both small and great, rich and poor, free and bond, to receive a mark in their right hand, or in their foreheads: and that no man might buy or sell, save he that had the mark, or the number of the beast, or the number of his name. Here is wisdom. Let him that hath understanding count the number of the beast: for it is the number of a man; and his number is six hundred three score and six" **(Revelation 13:16-18).**

Here are three of the most wondered about and most discussed verses in the Bible. Many theories have been advanced attempting to explain the true meaning behind the number "666," the Mark of the Beast. Some explanations have sounded reasonable, while others have appeared to be far fetched, but a careful study of these verses does seem to indicate certain facts.

The "Mark" will probably be first required at the mid-point of the Tribulation Period, coinciding with the defilement of the Jewish Temple by the Image. It will be used as a sure means of identifying true followers of the Antichrist, and none will be permitted to buy or sell unless they receive it upon their person.

The Bible implies that the Mark will be placed upon people in one of three versions.

1. A symbolic picture or emblem.
2. The name of the Antichrist.
3. A number representing his name.

Any attempt to predict the exact appearance of the emblem used as the "Mark of the Beast" is mere speculation at this time. some have offered suggestions showing a degree of merit, but they are only possibilities at best. The Antichrist, in selecting a suitable mark, might employ a symbol representing a popular slogan, or a national organization. We simply do not know at this point. I do believe there will be a mark, but, beyond that, only the Lord in Heaven knows what it will look like.

In the past, it was presumed that the mark would be burned upon the hand or forehead by a branding iron, or written in some type of ink that would not fade nor be erased. Also, it has been suggested by some that the mark would be invisible to the naked eye, or almost so, and would require the aid of a special light to be detected. A similar method employing a non-permanent ink is often used today in amusement parks to allow a person to leave the grounds for a while, then re-enter without having to pay another entrance fee. In the last few years, thoughts have turned toward the use of a laser beam, placing a tiny, almost unnoticed imprint upon the skin which could be read by a scanning device, but would not mar the features. Lately, there have been theories advanced concerning the possibilities of very tiny computer chips, placed beneath the skin. Such a chip could hold a volume of data concerning the person who wore the device embedded in his flesh, and, with the aid of satellites, could even locate the individual.

According to **Revelation 13,** some will choose to wear the actual "name" of the last great dictator, for it is mentioned as one of the three methods by which a worshipper of the Antichrist may be marked. Of course, his name is not known at this time, for he has not yet been revealed.

The third version of the Mark of the Beast concerns the number 666. This is perhaps the better known version of the three. But while there is no mystery regarding what the literal number will be, the relationship existing between the number and the Antichrist does remain unknown.

There is a hidden reference to the number of the Antichrist contained in the time intervals of the Days of Noah. the period of time between the translation of Enoch and the Flood is 669 years. This interval, representing the time between the Rapture of the Church and the Return of Christ, is the number 666 with the third number inverted to form a nine. Only an age using Arabic numerals, as we do, could notice the similarity between the two intervals of time.

There are other "pictures" illustrating the Last Days which also use the values associated with six. The great image erected by Nebuchadnezzar **(Daniel 3:1)** was 60-cubits tall and 6-cubits wide. Goliath, the giant, champion of the Philistine army **(I Samuel 17),** was 6-cubits and a span tall; he went into battle with six pieces of fighting equipment—a helmet, a coat of mail, a breastplate, two leg greaves, and a spear. The weight of the spear's head was 600 shekels of iron.

These things seem prophetic of the Antichrist, a champion of the world against whom no nation will be able to stand. David defeated Goliath, and the Son of David will defeat the Antichrist!

The ill-fated alliance between Otto III and Sylvester II, who tried to form a one-world government a thousand years ago, also bore a hidden resemblance to the special number of the Antichrist. Sylvester II became pope in the year A.D. 999, which number, when inverted, becomes the number 666.

According to the Bible, the literal number associated with the Mark of the Beast bears a peculiar relationship to the name of the Antichrist. That is, **Revelation 13:17** seems to imply that the name of the Antichrist will bear a special numeric value.

This is not hard to understand when we remember that certain languages possess no special characters to denote numeric values in their alphabets. Most people are familiar with the method of writing "Roman" numerals. Certain letters of the alphabet are given number values, and are arranged in special ways in order to represent different numeric amounts. The Greek and the Hebrew alphabets also possessed no separate symbols to designate numbers. Instead, in these two systems, all of the regular characters bore a numeric value.

Some have even experimented with the English language, using the number six by giving the letter "A" a value of six, then increasing the number value of each letter by an additional six until all twenty-six letters possessed a number. Even in the English alphabet the number "six" seems to relate to man, for, by using this method, the word "Humanity" adds up to 666. But I suspect, since the actual nation bearing the brunt of the wrath of the Antichrist will be the nation of Israel, it seems only fitting that the name should bear the correct number in the Jewish language—or, perhaps, in the Greek language. But, by whatever method the number 666 will be revealed, we should remember that the name is only one of many clues by which the Beast of Revelation will be recognized. Those wishing to identify the Antichrist will have to wait until they witness the many signs personified in one person.

Chapter 13
The Great Tribulation and the Appearance of Christ

"Weeping may endure for a night, but joy cometh in the morning" **(Psalm 30:5).**

When the Antichrist destroys the organization of the Harlot Church, and places his own image in the Jewish Temple (or, if the temple has not been built at that time, the unholy image may very well be placed upon the grounds where the temple once stood), he will attempt to unify the whole world by establishing a new faith with himself as the god of that religion. The False Prophet (the Second Beast of **Revelation 13**) will be his high priest, and will perform miracles, causing much of the world to worship the Dragon through the Antichrist. But many will choose not to worship him, and the persecution spoken of in **Matthew 24:15-21** will begin. The persecution is also mentioned in **Revelation 12,** where the woman (Israel) is persecuted by the Dragon (in the person of the First Beast, the Antichrist).

Many people will die in these days, particularly among those of the Jewish race, for the hatred of Satan will be heavy upon these people. His ruthless vendetta is motivated by the fact that the Messiah was a Jew! **Zechariah 13:8-9** infers that two out of every three Jews will perish during the seven years of tribulation, but a remnant will be preserved.

"And the woman [Israel] *fled into the wilderness, where she hath a place prepared of God, that they should feed her there a thousand two hundred and threescore days"* **(Revelation 12:6).**

Some theologians believe that certain numbers of the Jewish people will flee into the wilderness of Judea, the severely barren terrain between Jerusalem and the Jordan where it flows into the Dead Sea. Here, in the same territory where Jesus fasted and was tempted by the Devil, they may find refuge for the last half of the Tribulation Period. Others believe they may flee to the south into the Sinai where

Israel once walked with Moses for forty years. Still others think at least some will flee to the rose-red city of Petra.

Petra is located in craggy rock mountains below the Dead Sea in Jordan. In the age of David and Solomon, this area was part of the land of Edom. The ruins of this once prosperous city are literally carved into the stone cliffs of the mountain sides, and the only entrance into its locality is a very narrow defile, called the Siq.

The Tribulation Period will be a time of great chaos and physical catastrophe, the forces of nature itself in uncontrolled upheaval. Men will groan within themselves with fear when they regard those things which are taking place, for their eyes have never seen conditions like these. The twenty-fourth chapter of Matthew tells of famines, pestilences, and earthquakes. The book of Revelation speaks of tormenting locusts with stings like a scorpion; mysterious demon-like horsemen who slay the third part of humanity; disasters at sea; and giant hailstones out of heaven, each weighing about 100 pounds.

"...or hast thou seen the treasures of hail, which I have reserved against the time of trouble, against the day of battle and war" **(Job 38:22-23)**?

These are not ordinary hailstones. Christ, in **Matthew 24,** speaks of the occurrence of "falling stars" near the end of the Tribulation Period. The two events could be one and the same.

Similar "hailstones" are mentioned in other parts of the Bible. In Exodus, a strange form of hail mingled with fire fell upon the land of Egypt **(Exodus 9:22-26).** In Genesis, brimstone and fire rained out of heaven as God overthrew the wicked cities of Sodom and Gomorrah **(Genesis 19:24-25).** When Joshua's army put the enemy to flight at Gibeon, the Lord cast down great stones from heaven, killing more of the retreating soldiers than had been slain by the Israeli sword **(Joshua 10:11).**

In the twentieth century, it is common knowledge that stones often fall from heaven. They are called meteors. Existing in untold numbers within the solar system, and perhaps far beyond, it is estimated that 100 million strike the atmosphere of the earth every day. By the grace of God, most are vaporized by friction before they reach the surface, but some do survive the fall. They are called meteorites.

The origin of meteors is not known, but many are definitely related to comets. Over a long period of time, it has been well established that at certain times of the year meteor showers occur with great regularity, when the earth passes through the orbital pathway of a known comet. Apparently, although the comet carries most of the bulk of material existing in its orbit, portions of the original nucleus have broken off during the centuries, and are scattered throughout the orbit.

The hailstones in Revelation are probably a bombardment of very heavy meteorites. The Law of Moses required "blasphemers" to be stoned to death. During the Tribulation Period this sentence is carried out from heaven itself.

The possibility of larger heavenly bodies colliding with the earth is also implied by the text of Revelation. Chapter eight, especially, mentions an object so huge that it is described as *"a great mountain burning with fire."* Immediately after this, an even larger body plummets toward the earth, and is referred to as *"a great star from heaven, burning as it were a lamp."*

We live our lives from day to day, believing that no major extra-terrestrial disasters ever occur, just because we have never witnessed them with our own eyes. But, the history and evidence of such happenings is written in the structure of the earth. A very large meteor crater is located near Winslow, in northeastern Arizona. It is 4,200 feet wide, and almost 600-feet deep. A larger one is found in the Ungava Peninsula of northern Quebec. In 1908, a giant meteor or shower of meteors fell in Siberia, and trees were leveled for a hundred miles in every direction from the point of impact.

The surface of the moon is witness to the sobering truth that extremely severe heavenly bombardments have occurred in the close vicinity of the earth. Such poundings of the earth's surface have happened, perhaps in a more limited manner, due to the earth's atmosphere, but the Bible informs us such collisions will happen with bitter results during the days of Jacob's Trouble. Many heavenly bodies are stored in God's warehouse of space, awaiting the time of their utilization—meteors, asteroids, and even comets. Some of the asteroids are known to travel in orbits which occasionally bring them very near the earth. In 1910, the earth literally passed through the tail of Halley's Comet. Of course, the possibility always exists that a wayward asteroid or wandering comet, completely unknown to astronomers at the time, will someday approach the neighborhood of earth on a collision course. Of course, to a Christian one thing is always certain—such a catastrophe will never happen to the world unless the Lord intends for it to happen.

Another intense happening will unfold during the course of the Tribulation Period. It is revealed in the sixteenth chapter of Revelation. Seven angels will pour seven "vials" upon the world. There are two opinions concerning these verses found in chapter sixteen of Revelation. One theory is that the seven vials are seven completely different acts, following one after the other in time. A noisome and very grievous sore will fall upon the men who worship the Beast and have his mark. The Greek word used in the Bible text signifies a running sore with highly offensive odors. This was the sixth plague brought upon Egypt at the time of the Exodus. It was also the form of sickness Satan chose to bring upon Job.

The Bible tells us the second angel will pour out his vial upon the sea (Mediterranean), and the sea will become as the blood of a dead man. The Bible does not infer that the water will be literally turned into blood, but shall become "as" the blood of a dead man—lifeless and corrupt. In **Revelation 8:8-9,** a third of the sea was turned to blood and a third of the life died. Here, all of the sea will be turned to blood and all of the life within it will perish.

With the pouring out of the third vial, the same plague that turned the sea to blood will then imprint its presence upon the rivers and fountains of water within the land. All water will become corrupt, and men will probably have to boil and purify water before they can have a drink.

With the fourth vial shall come great heat to scorch the earth and men with fire. The first interpretation of these verses requires that the radiant heat of the sun be increased. The mean temperature of the sun's surface is 11,000-degrees Fahrenheit. Man exists upon the earth within a very narrow temperature range. If there should be a variance of as little as 2-percent, life would die. Evidently, the temperature will not reach this extreme when the fourth vial is poured out, but conditions will be very intense and uncomfortable.

The fifth angel will pour out his vial upon the "seat of the Beast," and the result will be darkness throughout the kingdom. The light of the sun will be cut off for a period of time, and the temperature will plunge downward as the land gives up its stored heat. Bitter cold carries with it pain, and men will gnaw their tongues in agony.

When the sixth vial is poured forth, the Euphrates River will be dried up, apparently clearing the way for certain "kings of the east" to come marching.

The seventh vial will come during the closing portion of the Tribulation Period, and will precede a great earthquake, stones falling from heaven, and the destruction of great cities around the world, including Babylon.

However, in spite of these trials, men will not repent of their deeds, but will blaspheme the God of Heaven. Lack of belief plays but a small part in rejecting the Lord. Most men, of all ages, do so because it is simply what they choose to do.

The second interpretation concerning the seven vials suggest that the fourth, fifth, and sixth vials will actually happen at the same time. That is, when heat shall be upon one portion of the earth, darkness and cold will be upon the other part. There seems to be only one reasonable scientific explanation for this—that the earth stops turning upon its axis for a while.

This theory is not a new thing concerning the earth, for, according to the Bible, it has happened at least twice before. In the days of Hezekiah, a sign was given him by the Lord. The sign was that the shadow on the sundial went back ten degrees, or forty minutes **(II Kings 20:8-11); Isaiah 38:1-8).** This particular fact implies that the earth, influenced by a great force, was briefly interrupted in its regular daily rotational motion, and actually rolled backwards to the position it had held forty minutes before.

Perhaps this could have been effected by more than one means, for instance, the Lord simply pronouncing the word and making it so. But one physical explanation is a collision between the earth and a fairly massive body, or, at least, a close encounter with the gravitational influences of a large heavenly body.

When Joshua fought the enemy at Gibeon, and was prevailing, he desired the Lord to grant him more daylight hours, that the army of Israel might carry the battle through to complete victory. Joshua then gave an astounding order in the presence of his army.

"Sun, stand thou still upon Gibeon; and thou, Moon, in the valley of Ajalon" **(Joshua 10:12).**

Joshua's prayer was answered, and the Israeli army had its long day to complete its victory, but God brought it to pass in his own way.

The earth rotates about the sun, and the moon rotates about the earth, but day to day changes caused by these motions are not very noticeable. The daily east to west journey of the sun and the moon across the sky is actually created by the spinning of earth upon it own axis. Therefore, for the sun "and" the moon to seem to pause in their daily movement, and remain stationary in the sky, requires that the earth stop rotating. God could have performed this miracle by causing the close approach to earth by another heavenly body, or, brought about an actual collision at precisely the correct angle to interrupt the earth's rotation, then, natural forces takeover once more and the earth returns to its regular rotation movement. The heavenly bombardment by meteors at this time **(Joshua 10:11)** lends strength to this theory.

Needless to say, when the long day continued over the Holy Land, a long night continued over the other side of the world. Ancient manuscripts, found among natives in Mexico and surrounding areas when Columbus arrived, show that there was a time when night did not end for a long while, and, also a time, in another area, when the sun rose very slightly above the horizon, then remained there for a long duration.

So, in view of these things, all seven vials, spoken of in **Revelation 16,** could be related and unfolding at the same time, especially the fourth, fifth, and sixth vials. It is conceivable that the pollution of the waters, and the grievous sores, could also be caused, directly or indirectly, by such a bombardment of heavenly bodies from outer space.

If the earth should be halted in its daily rotation due to a close encounter with a large secondary body, or, due to an actual collision at just the right angle, heat would begin to build up on the daylight side. At the same time, stored heat on the dark side would continue to dissipate into space and the temperature would drop lower and lower. Therefore, one side would be "scorched" with heat, while the other side would be plunged into freezing darkness.

Since the Euphrates River will be dried up at this time, it is likely that the sun will halt over that area of the world. By this event, it is possible to approximate the part of the earth immersed in darkness.

A line drawn through the Euphrates River and continued to the opposite side of the world would pass through Alaska, part of western Canada, and the west coast of the United States. The twilight zone would include Australia, Japan, the east coast of Asia, Greenland, and a portion of south America (east coast). The night area would include most of South America, Mexico, Canada, and the United States. these facts seem to lend some weight to the theory that the kingdom of the Beast will be in the Western Hemisphere. these things probably will happen late in the seven years of the Tribulation.

"And it came to pass, when men began to multiply on the face of the earth, and daughters were born unto them, that the sons of God saw the daughters of men that they were fair; and they took them wives of all which they chose" **(Genesis 6:1-2).**

These verses from Genesis, which allude to an unusual event taking place during the Days of Noah, seem to describe a peculiar intermingling of angelic beings with human women. Its antitype in the last days before the Lord returns may be a devilish influx of occultism, spiritism, and demons, the foreshadows of which are already darkening the horizon. But the antitype may find its fulfillment in another means.

We live in an age of great scientific advancement, where our inventiveness not only affects the environment of earth, but has given mankind the ability to reach into space to other worlds. Man's thoughts have been focused toward distant planets and the possibility of alien beings, and television screens are flooded with many programs of space travel and citizens of distant galaxies. Surrounded by so many suggestions, mankind often finds itself asking the question, if alien beings do exist, do they also worship the same God of Heaven?

With these provocative thoughts in mind, would it not be a boost to Satan's goals to manufacture contacts between the people of earth and so-called "alien" beings? These "visitors" from another world would actually be the angels of Satan. They might deny the existence of a supreme creator, just as many humans do today, dragging others down in their unbelief. Or, they might throw their weight and support to the Antichrist, declaring him to be God come down to earth to dwell among men, thereby imitating the true Son of God. It is my personal conviction that Satan will not choose, or be allowed to use this particular method in the last days, but, since the possibility does exists, I have included it in the text.

The wickedness of men and the deception of Satan will be great during the Tribulation. But even in the ordeal of those clouded days, the true God of Heaven will send voices. The Bible speaks of Two Witnesses who will fulfill a special mission in the world during the last days before the Return of the Lord **(Revelation 11:3-6).** The length of their ministry will be 1,260 days, and will coincide with the great persecution brought by the Antichrist, which will last for 42 months **(Revelation 11:2),** and the woman (Israel) sheltered in the wilderness for 1,260 days **(Revelation 12:6).**

During the last half of the Tribulation Period, it will be extremely difficult to witness openly for the true God. The beast will have installed his false religion, and any person expressing contrary thoughts will have to face execution. So a night will fall upon the land when no ordinary man will be able to publicly work for the Lord. But God will provide special protection for the two unique servants.

"And if any man will hurt them, fire proceedeth out of their mouth, and devoureth their enemies: and if any man will hurt them, he must in this manner be killed" **(Revelation 11:5).**

For the period of time in which their ministry is in effect, no power will be able to harm these two ministers of God, neither man nor the devil himself. They will speak with authority for God, and will have God's strength behind them. They will be a conspicuous thorn in the flesh to the Antichrist, for, as he seeks to proclaim himself as god, his inability to muffle the voices of these two persons will declare very loudly that there is a greater power.

The Two Witnesses will declare the whole truth of God, but they will specialize in a very particular area—the Gospel of the Kingdom. This "good news" is distinctly different than the basic message proclaimed by the Church, which is the Gospel of Salvation.

The Gospel of Salvation is the story of Christ, the beautiful sacrifice upon the Cross, and the offer of spiritual rebirth for all mankind. The Gospel of the Kingdom is the announcement that the "kingdom" is near at hand; Christ will soon return from Heaven and will establish his throne upon the earth. This message was proclaimed by John the Baptist, and even Christ used it in the beginning of his earthly ministry.

The Gospel of the Kingdom holds special meaning for the Jewish people, for Israel will be elevated to the position of queen nation of the world, when Messiah comes. Both Gospels will surely he heard during the last years, but the Gospel of the Kingdom will be preached with imminent emphasis in the last portion of the Tribulation. It is this Gospel and time which is referred to by Christ as one of the signs to precede his Second Coming **(Matthew 24:14).**

The Two Witnesses are also referred to in **Zechariah 4:2-3,** and are there called the two Olive Trees. An exact identification of the two servants is not known, but there are likely opinions.

Some believe that the witnesses will be two people, already living upon the earth at the time before their ministry begins, but will be especially set aside for this task. Others think they will be Moses and Elijah.

The Bible does promise that Elijah the prophet will come before the great and dreadful day of the Lord **(Malachi 4:5-6),** and two of the miracles performed by these witnesses were performed by Elijah in the first chapter of **II Kings,** and in the seventeenth chapter of **I Kings.** But there are two opinions concerning the second witness. Some believe he will be Moses, while others hold that he will be Enoch.

Elijah and Enoch were the only two people in the history of the world who did not die at the end of their earthly lives. They were both "raptured" or "translated" that they should not see physical death.

Hebrews 9:27 says that it is appointed unto men once to die, and those who believe the second witness to be Enoch do so because of this verse. It is believed that Elijah and Enoch will return during the Tribulation Period, and fulfill their "one death." But the statement made in Hebrews 9:27 must be considered in a general sense only, for at the Rapture of the Church, untold multitudes of people will be translated in the same manner as Elijah and Enoch. These people also will never experience death **(I Corinthians 15:51-53; and I Thessalonians 4:13-17).**

Those who favor Moses do so because of certain miracles duly mentioned in **Revelation 11:6.** Moses had power to turn water into blood, and to smite the earth with many plagues. There also seems to be a reference to the Two Witnesses found in the account of the Mount of Transfiguration (**Matthew 17:1-9).**

In this particular series of events, there are several types and antitypes when compared with the last days. The phrase "after six days" seems to picture to us the approximate six Great Days from the Fall of Adam to the Rapture of the Church. The mountain top represents a heavenly place, and the fact that only a small portion of the total number of apostles is invited up pictures to us the Rapture, for the Church composes but a small percentage of the total population of the world. The three disciples saw Christ gloriously transfigured before them, just as the Church will see Christ in his glorified body when he returns. On the mountain top, Moses and Elijah appear, Christ speaks with them, and they leave. Some see in this an example of Christ, in a heavenly setting, speaking with Moses and Elijah and telling them that the time has now arrived when they must return to earth for a while, and carry out their special ministry during the last half of the Tribulation Period.

The work of the Two witnesses also proves the truth of **Luke 16:31,** for in the three and one half years that they are upon the earth, Israel will have the sure ministry of Moses, of a prophet (Elijah), and of those that have rose in effect "from the dead" **(Luke 16:27-31).**

Just as the three disciples sincerely relished remaining on the mountain top, the Church will desire to remain in the heavenly setting. But there will be more work to accomplish upon the earth, so, as the disciples followed Christ back down the mountain side, the Church will follow Christ at his return to the earth at the Revelation.

After 1,260 days, the Antichrist will be permitted to prevail against the Two Witnesses, and they will be put to death. The exact method to slay them is not revealed, but the Bible does foretell that their bodies will not be allowed burial. They will be left lying in a street of Jerusalem for all to see. It is obvious that the Antichrist will desire to make a public example of the two, for they proclaimed the God of Heaven in opposition to his own false assertion that he was god.

The Bible states that people of all kindred and tongues and nations will view their dead bodies for three and a half days. It would have been difficult for the "whole" world to witness the scene until the modern advent of television and the more recent placement of communication satellites in space. Now, we have large networks covering news stories throughout the world, and we only have to turn on our sets to watch history as it unfolds. Great rejoicing will break out around the earth, because the words of the two prophets had greatly tormented the people through the power of conviction. A sinful world can unite on only one thing, and that is rebellion against God. Herod and Pilate, who had been political enemies, became friends when Christ stood before them in judgment **(Luke 23:12).** It will be the same way at the close of the Tribulation Period. Men who have denied God and indulged in the wicked ways of a sinful world respond with hatred toward a light that exposes the true condition of their lives, and rejoice when misfortune seems to befall the source of their conviction.

As long as the bodies of the Two Witnesses remain lifeless in the street of Jerusalem, the Antichrist can continue in his false assertion that he is god, more powerful than any other claimant to that honor, and therefore deserves the worship of all mankind. But his public example will boomerang in his face! As the eyes of the world watch, the spirit of life from the true God will enter into them, and they will stand upon their feet.

"And they heard a great voice from heaven saying unto them, Come up hither. And they ascended up to heaven in a cloud; and their enemies beheld them" **(Revelation 11:12).**

The Bible relates that when these things shall happen, great fear will fall upon the people who view them. And, to add to the confusion of the world, the same hour that the Two Witnesses are transported back to Heaven, a great earthquake will severely shake the city, and seven-thousand men will be slain. The remnant will be afraid, and will finally give glory to the true God of Heaven **(Revelation 11:13)**.

These things will probably take place near the end of the Tribulation Period. If the 1,260 days of the ministry of the Two witnesses exactly corresponds with the 42 months of terrible persecution counted from the Abomination of Desolation, then the Two Witnesses will complete their earthly mission about one month before the visible return to earth by the Lord (1,290 days from the Abomination of Desolation).

The house of Satan has never stood united, save in its hatred for the true God. Satan is, in a sense, the father of rebellion, and all his children bear the nature of rebellion. It is surely to his dismay that they also rebel against him, if his power does not hold sway over them.

Apparently, certain "nations" of earth, though under the hard dominance of the Antichrist, will never cleave to him with great loyalty. They will sit and wait, seeking a chance to throw off his yoke, and assume for themselves the role of world dictators. In doing so, they prove themselves the true children of Satan, for that was the original sin of Lucifer (the original name of Satan), not wanting to serve the Lord of Heaven, but to overthrow him and take his place. Simplified, he did not want anyone else telling him what to do. So it would seem that at this time certain "kings of the east" **(Revelation 16:12)** will attempt to take advantage of the set-back the antichrist has suffered to his reputation, and the general confusion existing among the populace. Their armies will come marching into the Middle East.

Many things will happen during the last days of the seven-year tribulation. It will almost be as though all of the terrible catastrophes and plagues of the ages are brought together at this time, focusing on the period immediately preceding the Revelation of Christ. The world will not be without a final warning, for **Revelation 14:6-7** describes a special angelic messenger who will proclaim the "everlasting Gospel" to those that dwell upon the earth. This "gospel" should not be confused with the "Gospel of Salvation," or with the "Gospel of the Kingdom." The content of the angel's message is clearly stated by the Bible.

"Fear god, and give glory to him; for the hour of his judgment is come: and worship him that made heaven, and earth, and the sea, and the fountains of waters" **(Revelation 14:7).**

Jesus said that immediately after the great tribulation of those days the sun and the moon will be darkened, and the stars (meteors) will fall from heaven **(Matthew 24:29;** see also, **Joel 2:30-32;** and **Isaiah 13:6-11).** The cities of the nations will crumble at this time, including mighty political Babylon, which will receive the fierceness of God's wrath **(Revelation 16:19).**

The destruction of Babylon will come in one single day, being utterly burned with fire. Kings and merchants will bewail and lament for her, standing afar off. But they do not weep because they feel sorry for her, neither are they glad to see justice done. Their reasons are strictly selfish, for they realize that they have lost the main market for their merchandise **(Revelation 18:8-13).**

Caught between two mighty opposing armies of earth, the Jewish people see little hope for a physical deliverance. They surely will remember the messages of the 144,000, and the stirring sermons delivered by the Two Witnesses, and Israel will repent, and call upon the name of Jesus as Messiah!

"And I will bring the third part through the fire, and will refine them as silver is refined, and will try them as gold is tried: they shall call on my name, and I will hear them: I will say, It is my people: and they shall say, The Lord is my God" **(Zechariah 13:9).**

"And I will pour upon the house of David, and upon the inhabitants of Jerusalem, the Spirit of grace and of supplications: and they shall look upon me whom they have pierced, and they shall mourn for him, as one mourneth for his only son, and shall be in bitterness for him, as one that is in bitterness for his firstborn" **(Zechariah 12:10).**

"Ye shall not see me henceforth, till ye shall say, Blessed is he that cometh in the name of the Lord" (**Matthew 23:39).**

James F. Webb

War shields shall rattle; chariots shall rumble; weapons of war shall glisten in the fires of conflict; and armies shall come marching. And then…

"And then shall appear the sign of the Son of man in heaven: and then shall all the tribes of the earth mourn, and they shall see the Son of man coming in the clouds of heaven with power and great glory" **(Matthew 24:30).**

Chapter 14
The Golden Millennium and Beyond

"Blessed and holy is he that hath part in the first resurrection: on such the second death hath no power, but they shall be priests of God and of Christ, and shall reign with him a thousand years" **(Revelation 20:6).**

A few years ago, as I knelt in prayer before an open window, I looked up into the darkening evening sky at clouds rolling above the horizon. Being an artist, I often tried to visualize shapes and forms in those huge collections of water vapor, and I was not disappointed on that day. My attention seemed to be drawn to a particular formation which resembled a huge letter "J". In seconds, as I watched, the clouds changed in appearance to portray the general shape of a valiant white horse, with a rider upon its back. Other clouds, to the left and to the right, reminded me of multitudes of people following the mighty rider, and my soul thrilled within me when I thought of the fact that Jesus would someday return to earth in just that fashion.

"Behold, he cometh with clouds and every eye shall see him" **(Revelation 1:7).**

When he appears, mixed emotions will greet him upon the earth. The saved will rejoice with a happiness of great relief, for the appearance of the Lord at that time assures them of everlasting deliverance, the end of tribulation dangers, and the beginning of eternal blessings. The saved of heaven (coming with the Lord) will rejoice for happy reunions, the establishment of the kingdom on earth, and the fulfillment of justice upon those who oppose God.

But most of the world will mourn when they see that great and beautiful light appear in the sky. Kings, great men, rich, chief captains, mighty men, bondman, and free men alike will quake in fear, and desire to hide themselves in the dens and in the rocks of the mountains, for they will realize that the great day of His Wrath is come **(Revelation 6:15-17).**

In this world and age, maybe riches, wealth, power, position, and authority do make some physical difference in how people live. But when Christ comes in his glory, there will be no difference. There will be only two classes of people—the saved and the lost.

God is love, long suffering, mercy, forgiveness, and salvation. But there will come a time when a definite line must be drawn, and judgment must be carried out before that line is crossed over. It would not be fair or just for those who trust in the Lord, and suffer and bleed and die in order to remain faithful to him if there will not come a day of reckoning for those who reject him.

The Roman Sixth Legion was once stationed at Megiddo, for it was considered to have great strategic importance for it commanded the mountain pass between the plains of Sharon and Esdrelon. The Plain of Megiddo will also see a gathering of great armies during the very last days of the Tribulation Period. Some believe that sharp contention will have broken out between the different powers of earth, and that a battle is about to ensue between worldly armies just before Christ appears. The kings of the east have never liked the idea that a western power holds sway over the earth, and many believe they will come into the Middle East to settle the matter once and for all. Others have suggested that Satan, knowing the Scriptures and recognizing that Christ is about to return, will have gathered these armies to resist the Lord's arrival **(Revelation 16:13-16).** It is, of course, possible that Satan will use "disagreement" to transport the forces of earth to the Middle East.

Zechariah 14:1-2 seems to imply an attack upon Jerusalem before the Lord's physical return, the assaulting armies using Megiddo as a staging point. Darkness will fall upon the earth, and the armies will pull back to Armageddon (Megiddo) when the Sign of the Lord's Return appears in the heavens.

An angel will fly through the midst of heaven, proclaiming the Everlasting Gospel to those that dwell upon the earth, to every nation, kindred, tongue, and people. It should be asserted again that the message of the angel will not be the Gospel of the Kingdom. These glorious messages are reserved for men to utter, for only men have experienced them. The "good news", which will be announced by the angel, is quoted in Revelation.

"Fear God, and give glory to him; for the hour of his judgment is come: and worship him that made heaven, and earth, and the sea, and the fountains of waters" **(Revelation 14:7).**

God is about to set things right. The terrible years of the Tribulation Period are almost over, and Christ is returning to earth to put down rebellion, and to avenge the harsh injustices inflicted upon those who put their trust in him. The angelic message will be received with joy by those anxiously awaiting physical deliverance, but with fear and anguish by those who have accepted the Mark of the Beast. The book of Revelation proclaims some of the most solemn warnings ever spoken.

"If any man worship the beast and his image, and receive his mark in his forehead, or in his hand, the same shall drink of the wine of the wrath of God, which is poured out without mixture into the cup of his indignation; and he shall be tormented with fire and brimstone in the presence of the holy angels, and in the presence of the Lamb: and the smoke of their torment ascendeth up for ever and ever: and they have no rest day nor night, who worship the beast and his image, and whosoever receiveth the mark of his name" **(Revelation 14:9-11).**

One of the great focal points of history occurs at the close of the Tribulation Period, prophecy having foretold the event from early times. In **Daniel 12:6** the question is asked, *"How long shall it be to the end of these wonders?"* In **Revelation 6:10,** the souls that were slain for the word of God cry out from under the heavenly altar, *"How long, O Lord, holy and true, dost thou not judge and avenge our blood on them that dwell on the earth?"* The moment has now come!

"And I saw heaven opened, and behold a white horse, and he that sat upon him was called Faithful and True, and in righteousness he doth judge and make war...And the armies which were in heaven followed him upon white horses, clothed in fine linen, white and clean" **(Revelation 19:11 & 14).**

When Christ came to the earth over nineteen-hundred years ago, he came as a meek and lowly sacrificial lamb, not opening his mouth in his own defense. But when he shall return the second time, it will be as King of Kings, and Lord of Lords!

The Bible states that on that day his feet will stand upon the Mount of Olives, east of the old city of Jerusalem **(Zechariah 14:4)**. His angels will be sent forth to gather the saved of the earth into a physical haven of safety, and for the first time, the saved of heaven and the saved of earth will stand united together **(Matthew 24:31)**.

Jesus Christ will issue a battle challenge to the kingdoms of the world. *"Proclaim ye this among the Gentiles; Prepare war, wake up the mighty men, let all the men of war draw near; let them come up: beat your plowshares into swords, and your pruninghooks into spears: let the weak say, I am strong"* **(Joel 3:9-10)**.

The verses in Joel continue the challenge, commanding the heathen armies to come down to the judgment of God. *"Multitudes, multitudes in the valley of decision: for the day of the Lord is near in the valley of decision"* **(Joel 3:9-10)**. The harvest of wickedness is ripe, and the grim sickle of reaping is swung into the vine of the earth **(Joel 3:13; Revelation 14:14-19)**. Joel also mentions that this time will be a period of darkness, the sun and the moon and the stars withdrawing their shining.

God further prepares for the great battle which will soon follow by calling the carnivorous fowl of the earth to come to the scene of impending battle **(Revelation 19:17-18)**. This fact seems to explain the verses of Scripture found in **Matthew 24:27-28**. The carnage of battle will be so great that vast numbers of fowl will be required to cleanse the area of the dead.

An exact chronology of events relating to time intervals is difficult for this period of future history. Things will happen at a rapid pace, mounting up and overlapping in a series of occurrences unmatched in the ages of the world. But certain overall measures of time are given in the Bible.

The Antichrist will tread the holy city (Jerusalem) under foot for forty-two months. Then, rebellion will break out, apparently following the resurrection of the Two Witnesses **(Revelation 11:12)**. Possibly, the Lord will return to earth about thirty days later, or, 1,290 days after the Abomination of Desolation **(Daniel 12:11)**. But the full blessing and deliverance to accompany the Lord's Return does not seem to be realized until a total of 1,335 days have elapsed. During this forty-five day interval, we can only suppose that the saved of the earth will be gathered into a safe place, the challenge of battle will be issued, and the Battle of Armageddon will be fought. It is not easy to estimate the exact length of this battle. But, since it is apparently represented to us through the story of Noah's Ark (for this was the period of protection for the children of God), and since the actual rain fell for forty days and forty nights, when the length of time between the Rapture of Enoch and the time of the Flood is compared with the much shorter time between the Rapture of the Church and the Battle of Armageddon, the actual conflict will probably last for less than one day.

"And I saw the beast, and the kings of the earth, and their armies, gathered together to make war against him that sat on the horse, and against his army" **(Revelation 19:19).**

"Then shall the Lord go forth, and fight against those nations, as when he fought in the day of battle" **(Zechariah 14:3).**

War is a terrible thing, but not all who participate in a war are necessarily wrong. When God shall make all things right in the world, he will do so by using war. When men listen to Satan instead of God, and refuse to allow any other means to correct them, God has no choice but to put down that rebellion by war. But, when God uses this method, he does so in righteousness **(Revelation 19:11).**

During that time, he will be clothed in a vesture the color of blood **(Revelation 19:13).** Christ paid the price of sin upon Calvary, over nineteen-hundred years ago, but the scarlet garment he wears at his second coming will not represent the blood shed upon the Cross. It will represent the blood of his enemies, and will show that he comes with great destruction upon all that will oppose him. It will be the Day of the Lord's Vengeance!

Armageddon means the Mount of Megiddo, but also includes the plain of Jezreel and the great valley that runs through the middle of the Holy Land from the Mediterranean Sea to the Jordan River. It is approximately 200-miles long and 10-miles wide, but so great will be the slaughter in this terrible battle that blood will flow to the horses bridles, by the space of 1,600 furlongs (about 176 miles). In this battle, the most advanced scientific weapons of war devised by the genius of man will be matched against the simple spoken Word of God, and the Word of God will be victorious!

"And the remnant [of the army] *were slain with the sword of him that sat upon the horse, which sword proceeded out of his mouth: and all the fowls were filled with their flesh"* **(Revelation 19:21)**.

The hour of Judgment will also come to the Antichrist, the last tyrannical dictator, the man who had accepted the offer Satan had used to tempt Christ in the wilderness—the offer of rule over the nations of the world. The "beast," together with his miracle working false prophet (the Second Beast), will be taken prisoner by the power of God, and cast into a lake of fire burning with brimstone **(Revelation 19:20)**.

"And I saw an angel come down from heaven, having the key of the bottomless pit and a great chain in his hand. And he laid hold on the dragon, that old serpent, which is the Devil, and Satan, and bound him a thousand years, and shut him up, and set a seal upon him, that he should deceive the nations no more, till the thousand years should be fulfilled: and after that he must be loosed a little season" **(Revelation 20:1-3)**.

The power of Satan has been as a millstone about the neck of man since Adam and Eve succumbed to him in the Garden of Eden. But the fact that he can be bound shows that he is a person, not simply an influence or a principle of evil. This should be an encouragement to Christians. Men cannot defeat the Devil through their own power, but with the might of God he can be overcome.

Satan has been called the Prince of the Powers of the Air **(Ephesians 2:2),** the god of this world **(II Corinthians 4:4),** the Ruler of the Powers of Darkness **(Ephesians 6:11-12),** the Prince of the Devils **(Matthew 12:24),** and the Prince of this World **(John 14:30).** His position is so exalted even Michael the Archangel did not dare to insult him **(Jude 9),** but he is not omnipotent. Satan is limited, and when God declares that it is time for him to be imprisoned, he will be bound apparently without difficulty. In spite of all the bragging and endless but deceptive displays of strength shown by Satan throughout history, when it comes time for God's restriction to be placed upon him, only one angel is needed to carry out this task.

"Blessed and holy is he that hath part in the first resurrection: on such the second death hath no power, but they shall be priests of God and of Christ, and shall reign with him a thousand years" **(Revelation 20:6).**

Revelation 20:4 seems to imply that a resurrection will take place when the Lord returns at the close of the Tribulation, for, in this verse, John witnesses the souls of those who suffered martyrdom during the seven-year period, living and reigning with Christ through the one-thousand-year Millennium. This "quickening of the dead in Christ" is referred to in verse six as the First Resurrection.

The First Resurrection will actually be in two parts, just as the Second Coming of Christ will be in two parts—the Rapture and the Revelation. The first part of the resurrection will take place when the Church is "translated" out of the world. The dead in Christ, whose bodies have slept until this time, will then awake and be caught up together with the "living saved" to meet Christ in the air **(I Thessalonians 4:13-17).** The second part of the resurrection will coincide with the Revelation of Jesus Christ, when he returns to establish physical rule over the world. If the martyrs of the Tribulation are not resurrected, how can they reign with Christ through the thousand years of the Golden Millennium?

The Bible is careful to point out the blessed condition of the Saints who are included in the First Resurrection (embracing the resurrected dead, the Saints living at the Rapture, and those living and resurrected at the Revelation), for they will never have to worry about the Lake of Fire. the Blood of Jesus has assured them of eternal salvation, so all earthly woes and problems shall have vanished away in the light of everlasting security. It is a glorious thing to know that the "sin" question has been taken care of forever!

Soon after Christ has returned and enforced peace upon the inhabitants of earth, a great judgment will take place. It will not concern individuals as much as it will concern nations, for this judgment will not determine a heaven or hell destiny. It will determine the nations and boundaries that will exist during this

Millennial age. Nations of the world will also be judged in accordance with their treatment of Jewish people.

During the Millennium, there will be delegated power and authority throughout the world. The government of Christ will be organized and established, with high positions filled by immortal Saints **(Revelations 20:4),** but perhaps other positions will be filled by many of the Tribulation survivors from various parts of the globe. Christ will rule from Jerusalem, and the nation of Israel will be recognized as the queen nation of the earth.

The Millennial boundaries of Israel were promised by God many centuries ago as part of the Abrahamic Covenant. During the Trial of Nations, those boundaries will be proclaimed and fixed, and Israel will extend from the River of Egypt all the way east to the Euphrates River, and from Hamath in the north to Kadesh in the south **(Genesis 15:18; Ezekiel 48:1-29).** Students of the Bible refer to this vast territory as the Royal Grant, given to Abraham and his seed by the Lord.

The River of Egypt is not the Nile river, but a lesser route of water to the Mediterranean now noted on modern maps as the Wadi El' Arish. This seasonal stream flows from the mountains in the Sinai to the sea, its mouth on an east-west line through Kadesh. The entire area of land given to Abraham, and reaffirmed in Isaac and Jacob, is more than the Jewish race has ever possessed, or will possess until the Millennium.

"And the Lord shall be king over all the earth: in that day shall there be one Lord, and his name one" **(Zechariah 14:9).**

This is actually the answer to the prayer of **Matthew 6:10,** where it says, *"Thy kingdom come, Thy will be done in earth, as it is in heaven,"* It is also the time the disciples inquired about when they asked Jesus, *"Lord, wilt thou at this time restore again the kingdom to Israel?"* **(Acts 1:6).** And it is the fulfillment of the verses of Scripture found in **Isaiah 9:6-7;** and **Luke 1:31-33).**

The Millennial Kingdom will be a theocracy, that is, a world ruled by God in the person of Christ. It will be a perfect age in the sense that, for the first time, the government of the world will be perfect, with a perfect body of administrators. But the subjects of the kingdom will not be perfect. As long as mortal flesh continues to exist as such, there will be a degree of conflict between God and with the carnal nature within them, even though Satan will be bound, and no tempter will be present to deceive and lead the nations astray.

When Christ shall return to the earth and establish his physical reign, the great covenant verses proclaimed to Isaiah in **Isaiah 54** and **55** will cry out in fulfillment.

"Sing, O barren, thou that didst not bear; break forth into singing, and cry aloud...enlarge the place of thy tent...for thou shalt break forth on the right hand and on the left; and thy seed shall inherit the Gentiles...Fear not; for thou shalt not be ashamed...for thou shalt forget the shame of thy youth, and shalt not remember the reproach of thy widowhood any more." **(Isaiah 54:1-10 & 13; Isaiah 55:1-5 & 12-13).**

The Millennium will be a time which will witness great blessings upon the land areas throughout the world, as ecology is practiced in a true sense under the tutorage of the Lord. Man, for all his "civilized" ways, has disrupted the regular processes of nature for centuries, and marred the original creation of God by waste, carelessness, and disfigurement. When Christ ascends to the throne of earth, laws, and regulations will be enacted which will reverse these processes. The result will be that the world will blossom forth in a way not seen since the Garden of Eden (see **Joel 3:18; Isaiah 35; Isaiah 55:12-13).**

"There shall be no more thence an infant of days, nor an old man that hath not filled his days: for the child shall die an hundred years old; but the sinner being an hundred years old shall be accursed" **(Isaiah 65:20).**

Some teach that the lifespan of man will be greatly elongated during the years of the Millennium, and will compare to the very high number of years experienced by the men before the Flood. This theory is largely based upon **Isaiah 65:20,** which is interpreted by some to mean "if a person should die being only one-hundred years old, he would still be but a child." But there are two ways to interpret the verse, the second being that a child is guaranteed one-hundred years of life, after which he will reap the harvest of life, based upon his acceptance or rejection of the Lord Jesus Christ (for the unbroken chain of mankind, descending from Adam, will still need to be saved even in the Millennium).

Some people seem to have difficulty accepting the thought that during the Millennium both natural-mortal men and those who are clad in resurrected, glorified bodies will inhabit the earth together. But this difficulty should not exist. Jesus remained on earth for forty days following his resurrection from the grave. During this time, he mingled with and even ate with natural-mortal men. Certain angelic beings have appeared often to men in the Bible, and have not always been recognized as immortal. In those cases where the "visitor" was clearly a "glorified" being, it does not seem that any problem was present concerning their ability to exist together. In fact, when Christ led the three disciples to the top of the mountain, and was there transformed before their eyes into a glorified person, Peter expressed a desire to remain in that fellowship. The glorified beings will have visible bodily forms, fully capable of mingling with the natural inhabitants of earth. Any difficulty in adjustment will exist solely in the minds of mortal men, and should subside as the days and years roll away.

There will be a new temple constructed and used during the centuries of the Millennial Age, and it is described in **Ezekiel 40:1** through **44:31.** The particular rites and offerings to be performed in this temple are also listed in the last chapters of Ezekiel.

The land of the Jews will be divided among the twelve tribes of Israel as recorded in **Ezekiel 48,** and will show the tribe of Joseph separated into Ephraim and Manasseh as it was during the Dispensation of Law. The tribe of Levi will inhabit a central area set aside for the Sanctuary and the city. The portions given to individual tribes will run east to west across the Royal Grant, beginning with Dan to the north, then: Asher, Naphtali, Manasseh, Ephraim, Reuben, Judah, Benjamin, Simeon, Issachar, Zebulun, and Gad to the south. The portion set aside for the Prince (Christ) will occupy the area east of the portion set aside for the city, the Temple, and the Levites, and will extend all the way to the Euphrates River. So, seven divisions are to the north of the Sanctuary and the portion of the Prince, and five divisions are to the south. The area ser aside for the city and the

Sanctuary include the area of coastline now occupied by Jaffa (Joppa) and Tel Aviv.

The Millennial age is represented in the Great Week as the "seventh day," and, therefore, is comparable to a Sabbath Rest. It will be an age in which the inhabitants of earth will rest from the ravages of war, and the deception of Satan. It will be an age when the land will supply the provisions of the people, and none will want for anything he needs.

"Again the word of the Lord of hosts came to me, saying, Thus saith the Lord of hosts; I was jealous for Zion with great jealousy, and I was jealous for her with great fury. Thus saith the Lord; I am returned unto Zion, and will dwell in the midst of Jerusalem: and Jerusalem shall be called a city of truth; and the mountain of the Lord of hosts the holy mountain. Thus saith the Lord of host: There shall yet old men and old women dwell in the streets of Jerusalem, and every man with his staff in his hand for very age. and the streets of the city shall be full of boys and girls playing in the streets thereof. Thus saith the Lord of hosts; If it be marvelous in the eyes of the remnant of this people in these days, should it also be marvelous in mine eyes? saith the Lord of hosts. Thus saith the Lord of host; Behold, I will save my people from the east country, and from the west country: and I will bring them, and they shall dwell in the midst of Jerusalem: and they shall be my people, and I will be their God, in truth and in righteousness" **(Zechariah 8:108).**

"But in the last days it shall come to pass, that the mountain of the house of the Lord shall be established in the top of the mountains, and it shall be exalted above the hills; and people shall flow unto it. And many nations shall come, and say, Come, and let us go up to the mountain of the Lord, and to the house of the God of Jacob; and he will teach us of his ways, and we will walk in his paths: for the law shall go forth of Zion, and the word of the Lord from Jerusalem. And he shall judge among many people, and rebuke strong nations afar off: and they shall beat their swords into plowshares, and their spears into pruninghooks: nation shall not lift up a sword against nation, neither they learn was any more. But they shall sit every man under his vine and under his fig tree; and none shall make them afraid: for the mouth

James F. Webb

of the Lord of hosts hath spoken it. For all people will walk every one in the name of his god, and we will walk in the name of the Lord our God for ever and ever" **(Micah 4:1-5).**

Chapter 15
The Great White Throne Judgment

"For God shall bring every work into judgment, with every secret thing, whether it be good, or whether it be bad" **(Ecclesiastes 12:14)**.

Once established at the close of the Tribulation Period, the Kingdom of Christ will never end, even though certain physical changes will transpire. Nevertheless, there will be one more challenge to that kingdom, and it will come as the thousand-year Millennium draws to a close.

Satan, who shall have been bound in the bottomless pit for ten centuries, will then be released. He will promptly go out into the world, and once more attempt to deceive the nations of the earth. His intention will apparently be to gather them together under his power in order to make one last attempt at resisting and overcoming the Lord.

There are some who say that in desperation Satan will actually hope to win the victory against God, but others believe he will hope to use a psychological factor upon the Lord. The Devil is fully aware of Bible prophecy, and the many references to the Golden Millennium, the glorious kingdom age. He will also realize how close that period will be to the Lord's heart.

When Satan leads his army to threaten the camp of the Saints and Jerusalem, the army will be composed of a large percentage of the subjects of the Great Millennial Kingdom—*"the number of whom is as the sand of the sea"* **(Revelation 20:9)**. Satan's hope, according to the second theory, is that God will have compassion on the great army, and will not destroy its members. Therefore, failure to carry out judgment on that army will make it unjust to carry out judgment on him. But God is just, and where the Blood of Jesus has been refused, sinners must pay the price of their rebellion.

The willingness of great multitudes to follow after Satan, when he is released at the close of the Millennium, shows that "belief in the existence of God" is but a small factor in the failure of most men to accept the Lord. For, in the Millennium, there can be no doubt that

God exists. A physical and visible Christ will have sat upon the throne of the world for one-thousand years. All will have seen him, and all will have beheld his power and might. Yet, very many will join Satan in rebellion against the Lord. This implies that the primary reason men refuse to accept Jesus Christ as their own personal Savior is simply that they do not want to.

This was the original sin of Satan when, as Lucifer, he was lifted up with pride and chose to rebel against the God of all Creation **(Ezekiel 28:17; Isaiah 14:12-14).** He simply did not want anyone to tell him what to do, and he wanted no one to be above him in authority. In other words, he wanted to be the god of his own existence. Without the Rebirth through the Holy spirit, men are the children of Satan **(John 8:44),** and have inherited his pride and lust and rebellious nature.

Satan has been very persistent in his warfare throughout the ages of earth's history. He has made earth and air the scene of his tireless activity **(Ephesians 2:2; I Peter 5:8).** After the creation of man, Satan entered into the serpent **(Genesis 3:1),** and, beguiling Eve by his subtlety, secured the downfall of Adam, and, through him, the downfall of the race and the entrance of sin into the world of men **(Romans 5:12-14).** Before Christ was born, Satan tried by every means to prevent his miraculous birth—from corruption of the human race to the extermination of the line through which Christ would be born. He fought against Christ while the Lord was upon the earth, and then, since the Cross, he has attempted to warp, to discredit, and destroy the truth of God's word, and to prevent it from saving the lost. Through the centuries, Satan has had excess to before the Throne of God, and what time he has not been in the earth, warring against God's people, he has been in heaven, accusing them before God.

In the middle of the Tribulation Period, he will be cast out of heaven, and permitted to go there no more. He will come down to earth having great wrath. With the Antichrist and the False Prophet, he will carry on a terrible persecution during the last half of the seven years of tribulation, setting up his own system of religion, and compelling the world to worship him through the Antichrist. As a result of Christ's great victory at the Battle of Armageddon, the

Antichrist and the False Prophet will be cast into the Lake of fire, and Satan will be bound a thousand years in the bottomless pit.

When he is released at the close of the Millennial Age, he will once more deceive the nations, and will recruit a great army in opposition to the Lord. Satan is the great deceiver. He will cause the inhabitants of the world to think unsound thoughts, and they will again imagine a vain thing **(Psalm 2),** that they can be successful in their insurrection against God.

"And they went up on the breadth of the earth, and compassed the camp of the saints about, and the beloved city: and fire came down from God out of heaven, and devoured them. And the devil that deceived them was cast into the lake of fire and brimstone, where the beast and the false prophet are, and shall be tormented day and night for ever and ever" **(Revelation 20:9-10).**

Some say that hell is not eternal, and that those who are thrown into this place will not suffer forever, but are simply destroyed. However, in these verses we see that a thousand years after the Antichrist and the False Prophet are cast into the Lake of fire, they are still there. furthermore, verse ten speaks clearly of torment, which will continue both day and night, and will last for ever and ever.

"And I saw a great white throne, and him that sat on it, from whose face the earth and the heaven fled away; and there was found no place for them" **(Revelation 20:11).**

This is the final judgment, coming at a point in history between the Millennium and Eternity. Most references by people to the "Day of Judgment" or "Doomsday" are really allusions to this time. But the Bible actually speaks of several different main judgments.

1. Judgment of Sin (at the Cross).
2. Believer's Self-Judgment (throughout a Christian's life).
3. Judgment Seat of Christ (for the Redeemed—takes place after the Rapture of the Church).
4. Judgment of Israel (the Tribulation Period).
5. Judgment of the Nations (at the beginning of the Millennium).

6. Judgment of Satan and his angels (at the close of the Millennium).
7. Great White Judgment (after the close of the Millennium).

The physical location of the Great White Throne Judgment is not known with certainty. It will not be upon the earth, for we are told in Revelation 20:11 that the earth and the heaven have fled away (many believe that here the word "heaven" is used to denote only that portion of space surrounding earth).

The final judgment will apparently transpire somewhere else in God's immense creation. It will surely be among the "heavens," but probably not floating in space or among vaporous clouds, for **Revelation 20:12** describes the "judged" as standing (not floating) before the throne. The required area will have to be very vast in order to contain the billions composing the human race. We can only speculate on this point, but it is possible that somewhere in the Lord's universe there exists a predestined planet, prepared and waiting to be the scene of this great trial. Why not the present throne of God in Heaven? It may be so.

Jesus Christ will be the judge who sits upon that throne, as the representative of God the Father. *"The Father judgeth no man, but hath committed all judgment unto the Son"* **(John 5:22).** He is worthy for he has purchased the world and mankind by shedding his own blood **(Revelation 5:9; I Corinthians 6:19b-20a).**

Those who will gather before the Great White Throne and face the final judgment of God will be people who are classified as part of the Second Resurrection. They are the "lost" of all ages.

Since the Garden of Eden, the bodies of those who have died without Christ have remained in the grave. They will remain there until the close of the Millennial age, at which time they will be resurrected to face the White Throne Judgment. It will not be so for the "saved," for their bodies will be either resurrected or translated in the First Resurrection, a thousand years earlier. The souls of the "lost" (at death) have gone to hell throughout the ages, as typified by the rich man in **Luke 16:19-31.** These souls will be brought forth and reunited with the body at the close of the Millennium.

The souls of the "saved," between the Garden of Eden and the Cross, went to a place called Paradise. Its location was not in heaven. but within sight of hell, a great gulf being fixed between the two. The price of sin had not yet been paid. But when Christ died upon the Cross of Calvary, all debts were wiped clean for those who had put their trust in the God of Heaven. A multitude of souls came forth from now vacant chamber, as Paradise was moved from earth to heaven. that Paradise was once located in the earth but now placed in heaven is shown by **I Samuel 28:11-15 and II Corinthians 12:4.**

Some believe that those persons who were saved during the Millennium will also stand in the Great White Throne Judgment. Others believe that these persons, having accepted the Lord as Savior, and having reached an age determined by God, will have experienced "translation" like the living Saints at the Rapture.

It is possible that the name of every person who has ever lived will be included in the roll call at this judgment. But, if this is so, the saved will not have to answer for themselves. Jesus Christ himself will answer from the Great White Throne, and say in effect, "This person has trusted in me as his own personal Savior. His soul has been cleansed by my blood, and his sins have been washed away forever. His name is written in the Lamb's Book of Life!"

"And I saw the dead, small and great, stand before God; and the books were opened: and another book was opened, which is the book of life: and the dead were judged out of those things which were written in the books, according to their works" **(Revelation 20:12).**

The Book of Life contains the name of every person who has entered into "eternal" life by the redemptive power of the blood of Christ. For these people, there is no fear of the Lake of Fire. The Book of Life, a witness to the saving power of the blood of Christ, and to those who have trusted in Christ, is the chief evidence to determine a heaven or hell destiny. But there are other books mentioned which will be used in this judgment.

The "other" book which was opened was apparently the same as the "Book of Remembrance" referred to in **Malachi 3:16.** It apparently contains the individual records of every person's life. Every deed, every thought, and every idle word are recorded here, and must be accounted for. We can only try to imagine the size of a library so vast that it is able to hold a fantastically accurate account of all the billions of people that have ever lived. But god may use a different type of book than man. I once saw the entire sixty-six books of the Bible reduced in size so small that they were contained on a single card no larger than a page from a regular book. That was several years ago. Today, methods are available that can store enormous volumes and information on an even smaller scale. We live in the highly advanced age of space technology, where computers store tomes of data on chips. If man can do this, how much more must God be able to do.

"But I say unto you, that every idle word that men shall speak, they shall give account thereof in the day of judgment" **(Matthew 12:36)**.

There are only two divisions of man before the throne of God—the saved and the lost. But within each division, men will be judged according to their works. At the Judgment Seat of Christ, the saved will be judged for their works to determine the degree of reward. At the Great White Throne Judgment, the lost will be judged for their works to determine the degree of punishment.

"And that servant, which knew his Lord's will, and prepared not himself, neither did according to his will, shall be beaten with many stripes. But he that knew not, and did commit things worthy of stripes, shall be beaten with few stripes. For unto whomsoever much is given, of him shall be much required" **(Luke 12:47-48)**.

"And death and hell were cast into the lake of fire. This is the second death. And whosoever was not found written in the book of life was cast into the lake of fire" **(Revelation 20:14-15)**.

The everlasting Lake of fire is a very physical place, and is the eternal destiny of those who have rejected God and the saving power of the sacrifice of Jesus Christ. It is also referred to in the twentieth and the twenty-first chapters of Revelation as the "second death." The first death is physical at the end of life.

"It is appointed unto men once to die, but after this the judgment" **(Hebrews 9:27)**.

Revelation 20:14 shows that death and hell will also be cast into the Lake of Fire at this time. From then on, none will die throughout the eons of eternity, for death has been done away with. The fact that hell (a spiritual place of torment, for only souls go there) will be united with the Lake of fire (physical) is clear evidence that the final abode of the lost will be a place of suffering for both the soul and the body.

Some men refuse to believe in a literal lake burning with fire, saying that such a place is simply the figment of fanatical imagination, and could not really exist. But the opposite is true. While I do not claim to know the location of the actual Lake of Fire mentioned in God's word, I do know with surety that such places do exist in God's creation. One such lake of fire exists fairly close to the earth even now—the SUN! Keep in mind that the Lake of Fire will already be in existence at the close of the Tribulation Period, and the beginning of the Great Millennium, for the Antichrist and the False Prophet will be cast into it at that time **(Revelation 19:20)**. It is interesting to note that the portion of **Revelation 19** dealing with the Battle of Armageddon begins with an angel standing in the sun, as if to forewarn of the fate awaiting those who rebel against God.

"And they shall go forth, and look upon the carcasses of the men that have transgressed against me: for their worm shall not die, neither shall their fire be quenched; and they shall be an abhorring unto all flesh" **Isaiah 66:24)**.

At the end of the thousand years of the Golden Millennium, the earth will pass through the greatest cataclysm in its history.

"And when the thousand years are expired, Satan shall be loosed out of his prison, and shall go out in the four quarters of the earth, Gog and Magog, to gather them together to battle: the number of whom is as the sand of the sea. And they went up on the breadth of the earth, and compassed the camp of the saints about, and the beloved city: and fire came down from God out of heaven, and devoured them" **(Revelation 20:7-9)**.

"But the day of the Lord will come as a thief in the night; in the which the heavens shall pass away with a great noise, and the elements shall melt with fervent heat, the earth also and the works that are therein shall be burned up" **(II Peter 3:10)**.

Some teach that the present earth, along with the entire universe, will be destroyed, and a new creation be formed to take its place.

However, many others believe the biblical description applies only to the earth, and the atmosphere surrounding it.

The Jews recognized the existence of at least three heavens. Modern theologians interpret them to be either: (1) atmospheric heaven, (2) starry heaven, (3) God's abode; or, (1) atmospheric heaven, (2) area of the solar system, (3) the universe. Whether or not there is agreement concerning the physical division of the three heavens, the fact does seem apparent that the Bible does recognize more than one place known as heaven.

The Bible does not tell us the exact method God will use to accomplish his will upon the present earth, but there are several theories advanced by man. some, while perhaps possible, lack scientific evidence to back them, but there is one theory which seems to have ample scientific backing. It is the theory that the sun may someday turn into a Nova.

According to modern science, the theory that a nova is a "new" star is now thought to be entirely untrue. Neither are they "Temporary" stars, which was once believed, due to the fact that they are usually seen for only a short period of time. They are believed to be stars, already in existence, which, for some stark reason, suddenly flare up to amazing brilliance. This extreme release of energy is maintained for a while, after which the stars fade to their formal, or lesser, obscurity.

It has been shown that a typical nova may increase its brightness 70,000 to 80,000 times, and become a very splendid object in the skies. Sometimes, although rare, a Super-nova occurs, such as Tycho's star of A.D. 1572. These are usually seen in other galaxies, and outshine the very systems they belong to, which simply means, for a short period of time, they emit more light than millions of other stars about them.

Several recordings of novae are found in ancient history, and in modern times. A luminous nova appeared in the constellation of Aquila in A.D. 1918. Other sightings have occurred in A.D. 1901, 1934, 1942, and 1960. Even more recent appearances have been studied at length by astronomers.

Spectroscopic study of novae indicates a vast and terrific outward rush of incandescent gases takes place, probably caused by a titanic explosion with the star. A suggestion is made that the outer strata of the star suddenly gets beyond control of the gravitational attraction, and that the possible cause lies with an increase of light pressure from the center of the star, which is probably unstable.

Regarding the severity of such an exploding star, if our sun should become a nova, the earth and all the planet's would be melted, or instantly turned into a thin gas, depending upon the intensity of the blast. It would happen in the twinkling of an eye, so quickly that no one would have time to realize what was taking place.

Nova come in various sizes, from super to moderate. I do not know the exact rating of our own "star" but most scientist believe that the chance of a star becoming an ordinary nova once during its total life period is fairly high. Could this be the means chosen by God to bring about the results described in the book of Revelation? In view of the scope of destruction in that happening, it is entirely possible.

There are two theories concerning the extent of devastation to befall the earth at this time, One theory holds that the earth will be completely destroyed, and a new creation take its place. The other theory believes in a lesser catastrophe, resulting in a renovated earth; the same world existing into the years of endless eternity, but purified by the fire of the Lord.

In some ways, this theory concerning the earth is similar to the saved man who is glorified and made perfect by the power of God. In such a case regarding the earth, the exterior surface would be changed. All that sin has brought into existence would be destroyed—thorns, thistles, disease, and works of man. It is, perhaps, significant that the Greek word "parerchomai," used in **Revelation 21:1,** and translated "pass away," actually means to pass from one existence to another. We are told that matter is never really destroyed, but passes into a different form. It is possible that this present earth, renovated, melted, and remolded by the hand of God, will be the new world, witnessed by John as the eternal home of the Redeemed.

James F. Webb

Chapter 16
The Eternal City and the New World

"And I saw a new heaven and a new earth: for the first heaven and the first earth were passed away; and there was no more sea" **(Revelation 21:1)**

Some envision this verse to mean a world completely covered by dry land, but this is not necessarily so. To the Jew, the sea meant a separation, the land divided as are continents, countries, islands, and so forth. Therefore, the verse is satisfied by the theory that all land area will be together in one mass, and that there will be one great ocean. This is the Continental Drift theory in reverse.

It is an increasingly accepted belief that, originally, all land area was together, comprising one great continent. If we look at a map, many portions of the continents do seem to possess edges which are compatible to other masses of land, something like pieces of a giant jig-saw puzzle with the edges worn and dulled by time. Chemicals, mineral deposits, fossils, and even types of plant life have been shown to largely correspond with "matching" pieces of the puzzle.

The outer crust of the earth is extremely thin in places, and is subject to stress along with the underlying mantle. According to the Continental Drift Theory, there was a time, in the history of the earth, when the largely singular mass of land split apart and drifted upon the earth's ever changing surface. Very careful measurements indicate that this movement is still continuing at a slow rate even today, as material rises between the plates in the ocean floor, forcing the crust to spread further apart. It is a picture of a world "broken" by sin.

It seems almost logical that the eternal earth should be one great world: united in Christ, united in government, united in cause, and united once again in one great land mass.

Very little is revealed by the Bible concerning the physical features of the new world, but in **Revelation 21:10,** John is carried to the top of a high mountain, from which he witnesses the descent of the Holy City. If John, though only in spirit, is allowed to stand upon an actual feature of the eternal world, then we can suppose that the new world will contain characteristics similar to the old world, but in perfection and glorified.

In the present world, mountains and rivers are known to often present barriers to man, dividing certain areas of land and making travel difficult. But in that world, they will surely be located in such ways that they will enhance the beauty of the land. but never divide it. Eden was a beautiful place, a garden containing rivers and trees and pleasant conditions. There is no reason to believe that the new world will be anything less. In my mind, I visualize a world of rivers, lakes, streams, meadows, woodlands, fields, hills, and mountains, but beautiful and perfect—the true Promised Land!

In the twenty-first chapter of Revelation, the Apostle John is given a thrilling privilege. He is allowed to view the great and Holy City, the New Jerusalem, descending out of heaven to the world. It will be a unique city not made by the hands of man, but constructed entirely by God. It shall have been built in heaven, but it's eternal site will be upon the earth.

Some have ventured the theory that the New Jerusalem will never rest upon the new world, but will circle the earth in orbit as the moon does now. But I have never been able to find any proof of this theory. Perhaps the Bible does not literally say that the city actually lands upon the earth, but the implication is very strong. In **Revelation 21:22-23,** we are told that Christ will dwell in this city, for, he is the temple of it, and also the light. In **Revelation 21:3,** it is stated that the tabernacle (temple) of God will be "with" men, "and he will dwell with them, and they shall be his people, and God himself shall be with them, and be their God" If the city remains in the heavens, circling the earth, then God will continue to dwell in heaven and will not dwell with man. The new world will be inhabited and divided into nations **(Revelation 21:24-26),** and God cannot be with men on earth and yet dwell in the heavens above the earth. Therefore, it seems apparent that the city will literally rest upon the surface of that new and beautiful world.

"And there came unto me one of the seven angels...and talked with me, saying, Come hither, I will shew thee the bride, the Lamb's wife.

And he carried me away in the spirit to a great and high mountain, and shewed me that great city, the holy Jerusalem, descending out of heaven from God" **(Revelation 21:9-10)**.

In this present age, the Church is the espoused Bride of Christ, but, in that age to come, the Church will be the wife, and in this role, the Church will hold a very close relationship to the city. A home is not really a building, but the people who dwell in it. A city is not the structures, buildings, and houses, but the people who live in them. A church is not the building, but the people who meet in the building. However, we refer to the building as "the church." The New Jerusalem is referred to as "the Lamb's wife" because it is the eternal home of the Church. It is the place Jesus said he was going to prepare.

"In my Father's house are many mansions: if it were not so, I would have told you. I go to prepare a place for you. And if I go and prepare a place for you, I will come again, and receive you unto myself: that where I am, there ye may be also" **(John 14:2-3)**.

The New Jerusalem will be a truly beautiful and shinning city, for it will have the glory of God, and its light *"like unto a stone most precious, even like a jasper stone, clear as crystal"* **(Revelation 21:11)**. It will be a four-sided city, and will have a very great wall about it (216-feet, or, 72-yards high). The wall will have twelve gates, three giving entrance to the city from each side. Each gate will have an angel tending it, and each gate will have the name of one of the tribes of Israel inscribed upon it. This seems to designate the particular entrance people will use to enter the city.

When Israel camped in the wilderness, they were commanded by the Lord to arrange the twelve tribes in a special manner. At that time, there were three tribes to the east, three tribes to the south, three tribes to the west, and three tribes to the north. The tribe of Levi dwelt in the tabernacle area, and served in that capacity, being withdrawn from the regular twelve tribes. the tribe of Joseph was divided into two tribes, Ephraim, and Manasseh, in order to fill the spot vacated by Levi.

This seems to be a picture of the eternal world, with the twelve Jewish nations situated about the New Jerusalem in the same manner that the tribes of Israel were placed about the portable Tabernacle in the Wilderness **(See Chart 12)**. We remember the twelve gates and the names of the tribes of Israel inscribed over each gate (see, also, **Ezekiel 48:30-35).**

But what of the Gentiles who are saved after the Church has been taken out of the world at the Rapture? How will they fit into the new world of eternity? There will be many people saved from all nations during the Tribulation Period and on through the golden years of the Millennium. Unless they are incorporated into the twelve tribes of Israel, they will be a separate unit in the new world, for they cannot be counted as members of the Church. There are no new members of the Church after the Rapture.

In the seventh chapter of **Revelation,** we are told of a great multitude, which no man could number. They are said to be of nations, kindreds, people, and tongues. The Apostle John is told that these people are *"they which came out of great tribulation, and have washed their robes, and made them white in the blood of the Lamb."*

I feel confident that beyond the precious ring of Israel, the remaining large portions of land extending on to the coast of the sea will be made up of select nations which the Lord shall have chosen to exist in that the precious earth throughout the endless eons of eternity. The number of those nations and the identity of them is known only to the Lord. I can only pray that America, my own beloved country, might be one of them.

CHART 12
DIVISION OF THE NEW WORLD

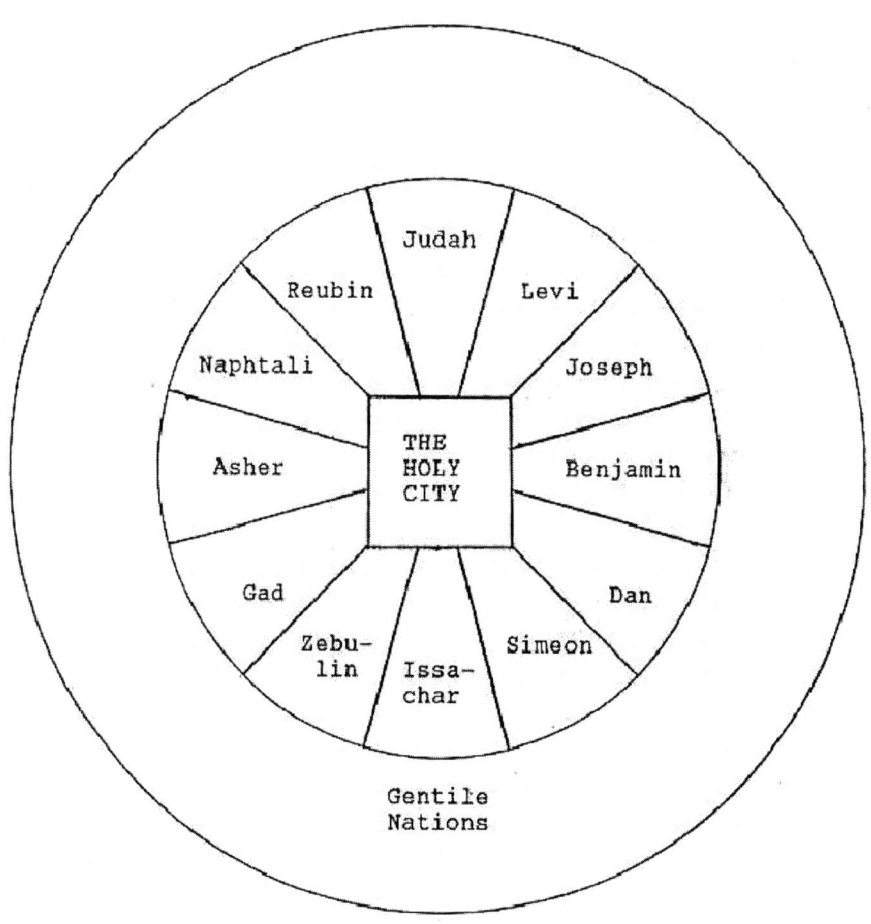

It is possible that the tribes of Ephraim and Manasseh will again be joined into the single tribe of Joseph, and Levi will be reinstated among the original tribes. In the prophetic picture, the Levites represented the Church, dwelling in the Holy City, but in the actual Eternal Age, the Church itself will dwell in that place. This offers the opportunity for Levi to once more take his rightful place among the twelve tribes. However, this is a matter of speculation.

It is interesting to notice that the small skullcap resting upon the head of the Jew—the "yamulka," traditionally worn by Jewish males on certain occasions—greatly resembles the land area resting upon the globe of the new world. It is believed that Christians will inherit the Holy City Jerusalem, while the Jews will inherit the world itself. In this sense, the yamulka is prophetic.

A city so great will need foundations, and the Bible records that there will be twelve, each bearing the name of one of the Apostles **(Revelation 21:14)**. They will be both very beautiful and impressive to behold, and will be garnished with precious stones, each foundation exhibiting a different type of gem. According to **Revelation 21:19-20,** the first foundation is of jasper; the second is of sapphire; and so on, the remaining ten using the chalcedony, the emerald, the sardonyx, the sardius, the chrysolite, the beryl, the topaz, the chrysoprase, the jacinth, and the amethyst.

Above the foundations, the great city will extend upward well above the atmosphere, if the surrounding mantle of air resembles the depth of the present world's atmosphere. There will be a spot within that structure to house every person who became a member of the Church when he trusted in Jesus as his own personal Savior. There is also a remarkable picture given to us in this very fact.

"Ye, also, as lively stones, are built up a spiritual house, an holy priesthood, to offer up spiritual sacrifices, acceptable to God by Jesus Christ" **(I Peter 2:5).**

"Now therefore ye are no more strangers and foreigners, but fellowcitizens with the saints, and of the household of God; and are built upon the foundation of the apostles and prophets. Jesus Christ himself being the chief corner stone; in whom all the building fitly framed together groweth unto an holy temple in the Lord: in whom ye also are builded together for an habitation of God through the spirit" **(Ephesians 2:19-22).**

Some imagine a contradiction in these verses, for **I Corinthians 3:11** seems to imply that Jesus Christ is the only foundation. But we must recognize what is being spoken of before we can understand properly.

Jesus Christ is the foundation of our faith. Without him, there is nothing, for nothing can endure if not based upon Christ. But Christ is the rock upon which the foundation rests. The four verses quoted above from Ephesians, refer to the organization of the Church. Christ came into the world to give his life that the price of sin might be paid, and, to organize the Church. He then entrusted the task of guiding that Church to twelve men, who were the apostles. Therefore, they became the nucleus upon which the rest of the Church grew—the foundation.

In Eternity, the New Jerusalem seems to be modeled after the organization of the Church, as an everlasting reminder of the Church's history. There will be the twelve foundations, declaring the twelve apostles; then, upon that foundation, the city itself, constructed to represent the individual members of the Church. If you are a saved member of the Lord's True church, somewhere in that wonderful city there will be a place with your name written upon it. Without it, the city would not be complete.

The Holy City will be far larger than any other city that has been known to exist upon the face of the earth. Its length will be the same as its width, and its height will be the same as its length and its width. The measurement of each dimension is 12,000 furlongs **(Revelation 21:16).** Therefore, since one furlong equals 660 (8 furlongs '1 mile), the height of the city, and the length of each side is 1,500 miles (12,000 divided by 8).

This is an immense city, indeed! If it were placed upon the American continent, it would just about cover half of the United States. A person, beginning a journey around the outward wall, would travel a distance of 6,000 miles before he would completely circle the city. The total area upon which the city would sit will equal 2,250,000-square miles.

The general shape of the Holy City is not known with complete certainty, but many believe that the reference in the Bible to its being "foursquare," implies that it will be cube shaped. But this is not necessarily so. Other verses from the Bible also show that the word "foursquare" does not apply to anything beyond the shape of the foundation, or the plot that the city is built upon.

Exodus 28:15-16 describes the breastplate worn by the high priest. the Bible verses say it was "foursquare," being a span in length, and a span in width. However, though it was bedecked by twelve jewels, it was definitely not a span thick. It was made of cloth and folded double to make a pouch, in which was carried the Urim and the Thummim **(Exodus 28:30).**

It has been hard to determine just what the Urim and Thummim actually were. Their names meant "lights and perfections" and they were used to ascertain the will of God in a way not delivered to us through the ages. Apparently, God spoke to the priests by their use, but how is a mystery. Whether or not the twelve stones of the breast plate were employed in some way along with the two objects is not known. There have been some serious theories put forth in recent years, and a few archaeological findings may lend support to those theories, but, at the present time, they seem to be too extreme and out of date for that age, so I will not mention them here.

Again concerning the matter of "foursquare." the brazen altar of the Tabernacle **(Exodus 27:1)** was also considered to be built in a "foursquare" design. It was five cubits long, and five cubits broad, but the height of it was three cubits.

It is apparent that the Holy City will have four sides, and that the plot of land occupied by the city will be square in its shape. However, the appearance of the structure above the land and the twelve foundations is still somewhat a mystery, except for the fact that it will reach 1,500 miles into the sky.

A cube does fit this description, but so does a pyramid. And a pyramid, architecturally speaking, is better suited for so large a structure. There are numerous verses found in the Bible which speak and prophesy of the "mountain of the Lord," and a mountain is very much like a pyramid.

Ephesians 2:19-22, quoted earlier in this chapter, refers to Jesus Christ as the *"chief corner stone."* A cube has a total of eight corner stones, four at the bottom and four at the top. It is probable that one stone would be laid into place before the others, but, when all eight are once positioned, all are of equal importance. But the design of a pyramid is different. A pyramid with four sides has a total of five corners, four at the ground level, and one at the apex. the four corners at foundation level are of equal importance, each touching two sides and the base (if the base is counted in the comparison). But, the stone placed at the "apex" of the pyramid looks down upon the whole structure and touches four sides, therefore qualifying it as the "chief" corner stone (see **Chart 13).**

"The stone which the builders refused is become the hear of the corner" **(Psalm 118:22).**

"Ye also, as lively stones, are built up a spiritual house, an holy priesthood, to offer up spiritual sacrifices, acceptable to god by Jesus Christ. Wherefore also it is contained in the scripture, Behold, I lay in Sion a chief corner stone, elect, precious: and he that believeth on him shall not be confounded. Unto you therefore which believe he is precious: but unto them which be disobedient, the stone which the builders disallowed, the same is made the head of the corner" **(I Peter 2:5-7).**

The construction workers, placing the stones of the pyramid layer upon layer, continuously by-passed one particular stone, due to its different shape. It was "disallowed" or "refused" by the builders. But when it came time to set the last stone into place, it was found that the regular stones, used in the construction of the rest of the pyramid, would not do. It was then realized that the "different" stone, by-passed from the beginning, was exactly the right size and shape to form the apex of the pyramid. It is possible that the magnificent New Jerusalem, the history of the Church incorporated into its physical features, will be pyramidal in shape.

The Holy City will be surrounded by a very great wall **(Revelation 21:17),** which will measure 144 cubits in height. This translates to a height of 216 feet.

CHART 13
THE CORNERS OF THE PYRAMID

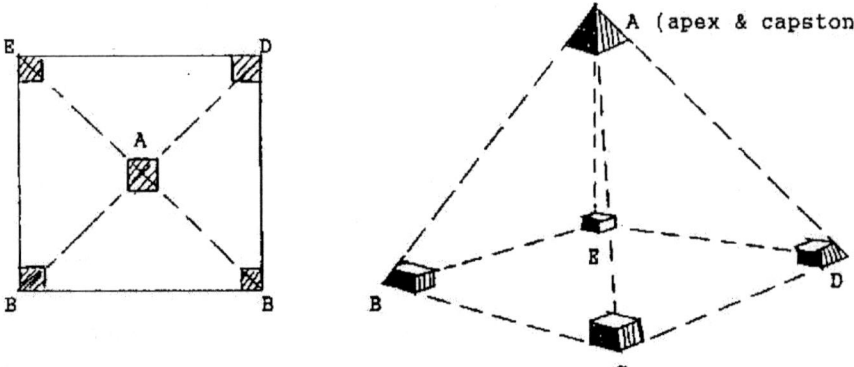

The four-sided pyramid has five corners, designated by A, B, C, D, and E in the illustration. Each of the four ground-level corners actually touch three sides of the pyramid (2 sides and the base). The corner, A, located at the apex, touches four sides. In this sense, together with its elevated position, corner A becomes the chief corner stone.

The New Jerusalem will be the most splendid city ever formed in the history of the universe, with its outside wall composed of jasper, and the structure of the city itself made of gold so pure that it is transparent, "like unto clear glass." The twelve foundations will be garnished with precious gems, and the gates in the wall will have the appearance of twelve pearls. The pearl, in the Bible, symbolizes the Church, so it seems only fitting that the gateways to the eternal home of the Church should be pearls.

The Bible relates that even the street of that city will be gold, and, as in the buildings, so [pure that it is transparent and "like unto glass," If the city should be pyramidal in its shape, there is no reason to suppose that the sides must slope steadily upward. The variety of designs God might use in his great city are really without number. But we can be sure that, whatever the exact layout may be, it will be the best designed and most beautiful city that has ever been (or ever shall be) constructed.

But it will be a city without a church building, a community without a temple. However, there will be a good reason. A temple and a church building are constructed as places to worship God in, but God at that time will be with man in person. The Lord God Almighty and the Lamb will be the temple of the New Jerusalem, and men will worship their creator face to face.

The Bible states that in that blissful place the sun and the moon will not even be needed, for the Lamb will be the light thereof **(Revelation 21:23).** The Lord is the source of true love, true life, and true light, and his glory will illumine the glass-like city throughout. When I think of that wonderful habitat, I see in my mind a glistening structure perfecting the aesthetic effect of a crystal chandelier. Some of the most beautiful sights known to man have been witnessed in ice formations silhouetted against a background of light, or in glass creations of art enhanced by the radiance of special lighting. The actual loveliness of the holy Jerusalem will surely be beyond the present attempts of man to describe it with ordinary words. But we will see it with our eyes!

"And the nations of them which are saved shall walk in the light of it: and the kings of the earth do bring their glory and honour into it. And the gates of it shall not be shut at all by day: for there shall be no night there. And they shall bring the glory and honour of the nations into it. And there shall in no wise enter into it any thing that defileth, neither whatsoever worketh abomination, or maketh a lie: but they which are written in the Lamb's book of life" **(Revelation 21:24-27).**

Life in the eternal city! The Bible speaks of nations, and kings, and glory and honor brought into the city (probably in the form of merchandise and harvest, for the eternal earth will be a world of plenty). The **"nations of them which are saved"** will be peopled by the saved of all ages, other than the Church. The inheritance of the Church lies within the city walls, for the members of the Church are not the subjects of the kingdom, but the adopted sons and daughters of the king. Those inheriting the land without the city are: those saved before the Flood, those saved after the Flood, those saved during the era of the Law of Moses, those saved during the Tribulation Period, and those saved during the Millennium.

A city that rises 1,500 miles into the sky will command an awesome view of the surrounding terrain. Under certain conditions it is possible that almost all the land area of that perfect world will be visible from the highest point. If the new world should prove to be the same size as the present world, and if the same approximate proportions of land mass and water surface hold true (to provide comparable climate and atmospheric conditions), and if all of the land area is gathered into one great continent, then some very impressive facts may be proposed. **See Figure 14.**

In this figure, the New Jerusalem towers above the land area of the earth. From a point on the surface directly beneath the apex of the pyramid, the everlasting kingdom stretches away in every direction for about 3,632 miles.

"And the nations of them which are saved shall walk in the light of it" **(Revelation 21:24).**

A light, shinning forth from the highest point of the city, would directly reach the land for a distance of about 3,029 miles. The principle of refraction—in this situation, light shinning at an angle through the atmosphere—would bend the rays of light so that about 69 additional miles would be added to this amount. This means that the upper most point of the city would be visible for almost 3,100 miles in all directions. This provides a directly lighted area enclosing nearly 30,152,000 square miles of land.

The remaining land (a large ring of about 534-miles wide and existing between the directly lighted area and the water) would lie in a zone of twilight, ranging from a condition to immediately after sunset to a time resembling our world about thirty to thirty-one minutes after sunset. Even at the shoreline, it would not be completely dark. See **Charts 12 & 14.**

This would provide additional usable land for each nation, and would greatly enlarge each country's total size. The use of the land beyond the directly lighted area is open to speculation, but would seem to lend itself well to service and industrial activity, if these things will exist in the eternal world—and there is reason to believe that they will

Behold The Bridegroom Cometh

(Revelation 21:24-26). This would leave the directly lightly areas free for residential settlements, agriculture, and beauty.

CHART 14
THE NEW WORLD

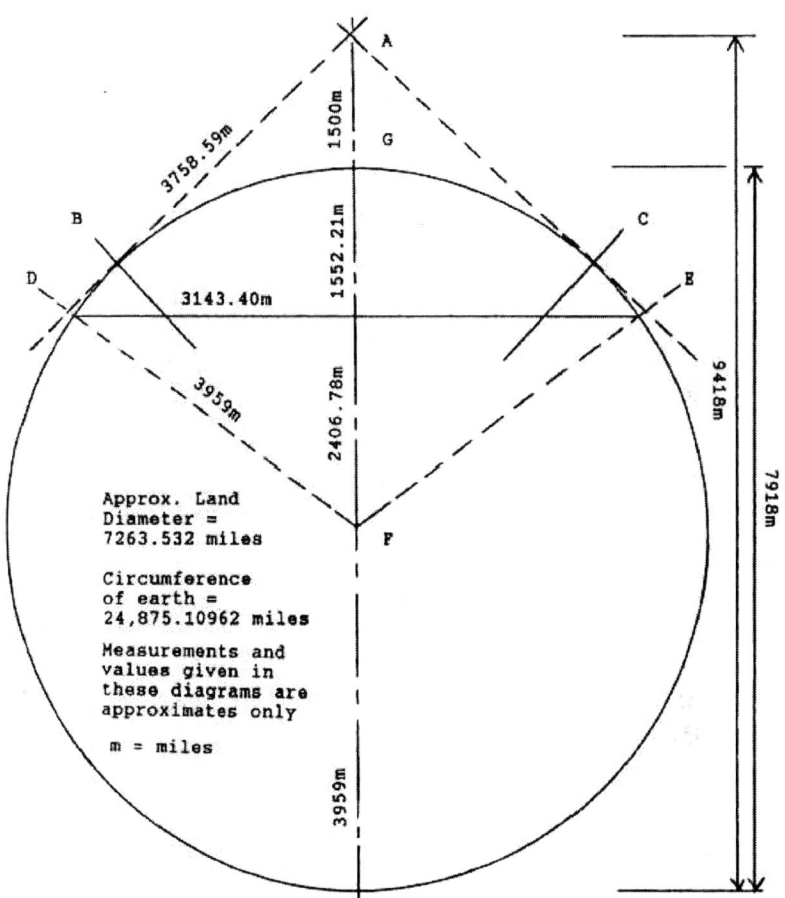

The small inset at the bottom gives an artist's conception of the Eternal World. The large diagram gives several important dimensions. Section DGED represents the land area. Point A represents the apex of the New Jerusalem. Direct vision from Point A reaches to Points B and C. Refraction of light allows direct vision even further, and allows a zone of at least twilight conditions all the way to the coastline.

In that world to come, the citizens will walk and live within direct sight of the Lord. They will know as they are known, and see no more darkly as through a dark glass **(I Corinthians 13:12).** We will behold the features of our Savior, face to face.

If the atmosphere of the new world resembles that of the present earth in density and depth, it will by no means reach even close to the upper regions of the Holy City. So it is probable that the New Jerusalem will be constructed in a manner similar to a mall, being enclosed above the atmosphere that it might maintain perfect conditions within. We seal our homes so they will be warm in winter and cool in summer. Airlines seal their planes so air will be plentiful at high altitudes, and also provide air conditioning and heating. Will God be less able to provide such facilities for his eternal children?

Such a city, with ports opening directly into space, would provide excellent embarkation depots for extra-terrestrial space flights. And those flights will surely come, for the God of that world will also be the God of the universe, and, as heirs with Christ of all things, the universe will also belong to us.

The Holy City of New Jerusalem is the fulfillment of a hidden prophecy contained in **Matthew 5:34-35.** In these verses, Heaven is said to be the location of God's throne, earth is referred to as his footstool, and Jerusalem is called the city of the great King. The Lord's throne, situated at the apex of the pyramid, will be 1,500-miles high, or, in space far above the atmosphere. But the foundations of the city will sit upon the surface of the earth, thereby comprising a footstool before the throne. And, the city of Jerusalem (the New Jerusalem will truly be the city of the Great King, the King of Kings and Lord of Lords!

The land area occupied by the Holy city will be immense in size, but, due to its great height, the inner volume of that vast creation of the Lord will have even more capacity. If the New Jerusalem should be a pyramid in shape, it will have an interior volume of 1,125,000,000-cubit miles. This volume is so huge that, if each individual person dwelling within that city should be given an area measuring a half-mile wide, a half-mile long, and a half-mile high, there would be enough room to accommodate a total of nine-billion people. This is much more than the present population of the world, and does not include those people living in the nations outside of the city. However, these figures have not been included in this study to imply the population of that great city, but, rather, to assure that there will be ample room for you.

"In my Father's house are many mansions: if it were not so, I would have told you. I go to prepare a place for you! **(John 14:2).**

Otherwise, if space were limited in that future city, and there would be room for only a certain number of people, the Lord would have warned us so we could compete with others and win a place. But those "homes" are not won except by the Blood of Jesus Christ. They, like our salvation, are completely free.

In the book of Revelation, John is shown an important river, flowing forth from the throne of God and of the Lamb. The river, among theologians, is known as the river of Life. Its waters are pure as crystal, not muddy or polluted as earthly waters often are, and, it is fitting that it comes forth from the very throne, for all life comes forth from God.

Its waters are perfect and clean, containing precious life-giving qualities, flowing through the Holy City and certainly blessing the lakes and streams of the nations of that world. It is likely that Christ referred in part to this same river when he told the woman at the well, *"Whosoever drinketh of this water shall thirst again: but whosoever drinketh of the water that I shall give him shall never thirst"* **(John 4:13-14).**

Chapter twenty-two of **Revelation** mentions a very special type of tree that will flourish in the New Jerusalem. It will be the Tree of Life, which was also mentioned in the Garden of Eden **(Genesis 2 & 3).** After the sin, Adam and Eve were driven forth from the garden to prevent them from eating of this tree and thereby living forever in a condition of separation from God. But, in that city to come, its fruit will be available throughout eternity for all to eat.

It is described as a marvelous tree which will bear twelve manners of fruit. Some interpret **Revelation 22:2** to mean that all twelve types of fruit will grow at once, producing a brand-new crop every month.

Others believe that the tree will yield a different type of fruit each month, producing twelve different types of fruit in a year, while others theorize the Tree of Life will come in twelve different varieties, each variety producing a different type of fruit.

It does seem to be evident, by the description given in Revelation, that the term "tree" (singular sense) refers to the species of plant instead of the number. That is, the name "Tree of Life" denotes a particular type of tree, such as: Pine, Oak, Willow, Apple, or so forth. The actual number of Trees of Life is not revealed in the Bible, but certain things which are given us indicate that there surely will be very many.

"In the midst of the street of it, and on either side of the river, was there the tree of life" **(Revelation 22:2).**

In some ways, I had always found this verse difficult, for I could not visualize a street with a river in the middle of it, and a tree, apparently split apart into two trunks, growing from both banks of the river. But I had not given the matter enough thought to understand what was actually being described. Then, one day, I remembered a particular street than ran through the center of Lawton, Oklahoma—the home town I grew up in—and I understood. Gore Boulevard is approximately a half-block wide. It contains a park area which separates the east-bound lane from the west-bound lane, and is decorated with a good number of trees and other plants. The park runs along with the street for several blocks, creating a stretch of scenic beauty right in the middle of the lanes of traffic. There is no river running down the center of Gore Boulevard. However, at one time, there were fish ponds, and, I suppose, just as easily, there could have been a river, if a large enough source of water had been in the proper place.

I believe Gore Boulevard is similar to the arrangement which will be present in the New Jerusalem. The golden street of the Holy City will be a great divided highway, containing a park in the middle of it. The park will be filled with the Tree of Life, and the pure river, flowing down from the throne, will follow its course through the park for the length of the street. See **Chart 15).**

I do not pretend to know the manner the river circulates through the city, whether it spirals down from the great height, circling about so that no location within the walls will be very far from the blessings of its water, and the beauty and fruit found in the park; or, if it expands into beautiful ponds or lakes, or cascades down different levels of the city in majestic water falls. I do feel that the scope of its beauty and reach will be beyond anything we have seen in this present world. And I thrill within me to realize even for a moment the endless number of ways that River could be treated and handled by the hand of God. When we try to visualize it, we must remember that we are not talking about the temporary world we now dwell in, but in a new, glorious world created anew by the master of the universe. Our feeble minds can not begin to fathom the dimensions of his ability.

Within the vast volume of the city's inner structure, it is surely true that there will be many lesser avenues, streets, beautiful halls, apartments, gardens, meadows, and provisions suitable for the eternal physical home of Christ—and the Church.

CHART 15
THE STREET, THE RIVER, AND THE TREE OF LIFE

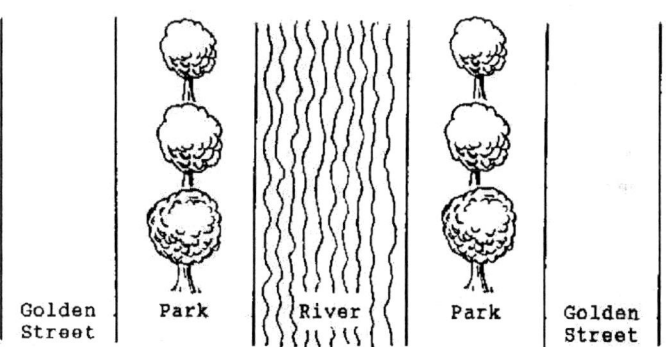

Revelation 22:2 seems to describe the above scene in the New Jerusalem. The River of Life comes forth from the throne of the Lord, and flows through the city. The tree of Life grows on either side of the river, and separate lanes of the golden street run along the outside boundaries. the scene is of a divided highway with a beautiful park, containing the River of Life, in the middle of it.

The new world will be a perfect world, the habitat of a pure civilization, created by God, which will see no sorrow, no death, no heartache, or physical pain. There will be no more frustrating disappointments or sad farewells, which so often plague the world that now exists. We will no longer dwell in mortal bodies, which slowly age and eventually see corruption. We will have glorified bodies, modeled after the very body of Christ—eternal, and with abilities far beyond the flesh of this age.

"But they that wait upon the Lord shall renew their strength; they shall mount up with wings as eagles, they shall run, and not be weary; and they shall walk, and not faint" **(Isaiah 40:31).**

When Christians speak of heaven, and the eternal home of the saved, this is what is actually referred to—the new world and the Holy City. And all who will live there will do so because they have chosen to go there. The decision will have been made in this present world—to accept the Lord by free choice. And the blessed of that "heavenly" place will be *"they which are written in the Lamb's book of life"* **(Revelation 21:27).**

What a wonderful thing—to know and cherish the fact that we are the children of God, and, as children, *"then heirs; heirs of God, and joint-heirs with Christ; if so be that we suffer with him, that we may be also glorified together. For I reckon that the sufferings of this present time are not worthy to be compared with the glory which shall be revealed in us"* **(Romans 8:16-18).**

"But as it is written, Eye hath not seen, nor ear heard, neither have entered into the heart of man, the things which God hath prepared for them that love him" **(I Corinthians 2:9).**

Chapter 17
Are You Ready?

"And at midnight there was a cry made, Behold the bridegroom cometh; go ye out to meet him" (**Matthew 25:6**).

The bridegroom is the Lord Jesus Christ, and he is coming back to the earth. This particular message has been proclaimed for many years, and we who are of the present generation have heard these prophecies all of our lives. But the multitude of signs concerning the Second Coming have focused together in this age as they have never done before. One does not have to read a single chapter of this book in order to see that the Return of Christ is very near, indeed—the Bible and history combine to declare it.

If a man believes the Bible, and accepts it as the literal word of the Living God, he cannot doubt that Jesus spoke of a visible, physical return to this world, to establish a great and wonderful kingdom, and to walk among and govern that kingdom's earthly subjects. It is the logical conclusion that the Bible story, from Genesis to Revelation, steadily moves toward.

In this book, we have discussed the surety of his coming. We have studied many differing facts and signs which imply that the return of Jesus to lift the members of the Church into the safety of heaven cannot possibly be very distant in the future. While we do not know the exact time table of God, we can certainly hear his warnings of the approaching storm of the Tribulation and the Last Days. It is my sincere prayer that those who read this book, though they may not agree with every thing I have taught, they will at least keep an open mind about these things, and that the Spirit of God will lead them to accept the book in its intended spirit. But, if you are among that number who do not agree with me in many of the things I have included in these pages, it is my prayer that you will at least believe that Christ will eventually return, that signs do seem to point to a not-too-distant coming, and that every person should live his life in such a way that he will be prepared to meet the Lord face to face.

"Wherefore we labour, that whether present or absent, we may be accepted of him. For we must all appear before the judgment seat of Christ; that every one may receive the things done in his body, according to that he hath done, whether it be good or bad" **(II Corinthians 5:10).**

One day soon, the eastern sky will flash with the glory of his presence, as Christ moves around the world, calling the saved people home. the Rapture is the glorious hope of the Church, and a deliverance from the harsh years of the Tribulation to follow. But only those persons who have accepted Christ before the time of the Rapture will be taken at that point. There will be people saved after the Rapture, but they will have to plunge into the Tribulation years together with the rest of the world. God will provide help for believers during the seven-year period, but many who stand up for Jesus will suffer and be killed for his name. What a blessing for the members of the Lord's body to be in the safety of heaven when those times unfold. And, also, because of the impending shadow about to cover the whole world, how important it is to win others to Christ, **NOW!**

Whether or not a Christian entirely believes the message as presented in this study, his basic work and form of life should remain essentially the same. If the Lord does not return for another two-hundred years, or if those who claim he will never return at all should be right (though I think they are not), it would still be just as important to win souls to Christ as quickly as possible. For life is shorter than most of us realize, and the years seem to pass by in a blink of the eye. One day, we look in a mirror and see a young person gazing back at us. Then, without warning, we awake to the knowledge we are grandparents, and many years have rolled by in what seemed to us only a few days. And the lost about us are still there, with so short a time in a full lifetime to save them.

The story of the Bible is based upon love. Because of it, man was created in the first place, his life was extended upon earth by childbirth after the transgression in the garden, and Christ was sent into the world to redeem the souls of men.

Love is a beautiful emotion expressed by one party toward another, but, to be experienced in its most blessed fulfillment, love should be expressed both ways. Therefore, it is one thing for a Christian to know the love and salvation given to him by God, and another to return that love. But it is only when love flows both ways between God and man that man is able to step up to a higher plain of joy and peace, and really begin to understand what life and eternity are all about. We love him because he know him, and we know him because we have walked and had fellowship with him. And in that fellowship, we seek to please him.

What was it that Christ said? *"Wist ye not that I must be about my Father's business?"* **(Luke 2:29).** And, also, *"My meat is to do the will of him that sent me, and to finish his work"* **(John 4:34),** and, *"for I came down from heaven, not to do mine own will, but the will of him that sent me"* *(***John 6:38).** It was in this sense that the life of Jesus was lived out while he walked the world two-thousand years ago. And the Father expressed his pleasure to the chosen group of disciples by audibly saying, *"This is my beloved son, in whom I am well pleased"* **(Matthew 17:5).**

When Christ shall return to the world, the Bible points out the blessed situation of the believer whom the Lord finds working—spreading the word and seeking the salvation of souls.

Now is a time to be sober concerning the things of God. In the present age in which we live, philosophers seem to oppose the truth of God and modern styles of living seem to ignore the things taught in the Bible. Apparently brainwashed by an age of pleasure seeking, many Christians appear very little different than the worldly people they are supposed to be trying to save. So many times, Christians allow carnality to become so prevalent in the habits of their lives that often they do not even recognize it as sin. They continue in those habits, wondering why they see so few people coming to Christ for salvation.

It is time for Christians to get serious about God! If we truly believe in him, and profess that the Lord is really the God that the Bible declares him to be, then it is time we begin to act like it, and to serve him in reality. In one way or the other, time is running out! Each day that passes brings us one day closer to a time when we can work no more. My prayer is that we will make use of every opportunity that presents itself to do the work of God.

"But when he saw the multitudes, he was moved with compassion on them, because they fainted, and were scattered abroad, as sheep having no shepherd. Then saith he unto his disciples, The harvest truly is plenteous, but the labourers are few; pray ye therefore the lord of the harvest, that he will send forth labourers into his harvest" **(Matthew 9:36-38).**

"And that, knowing the time, that now it is high time to awake out of sleep: for now is our salvation nearer than when we believed. The night is far spent, the day is a hand: let us therefore cast off the works of darkness, and let us put on the armour of light" **(Romans 13:11-12).**

It is my desire that every person in the world might in some way receive the message contained in these lessons—not because I thought them up and wrote them down, for I only copied them from the Bible, but, because they **ARE** from the Bible, and are true. I only hope that I have passed those words and truths on in such a way that others will be impressed enough by them to believe on the only true God and Savior, Jesus Christ.

The task of spreading the good news of Christ, salvation, and the possibility of his soon return must fall upon the shoulders of every person who has discovered the truth. We may not all be able to proclaim the Word of God in distant, far away places, but we can witness in the locality and situation in which the Lord has placed us. I believe that nothing really happens by chance, and that the God of the Universe is always in charge of things. We should never lament the spot in life in which we find ourselves, but we should look for the opportunity to glorify God by letting our lives speak of him before those around us. Tell others about Christ, about original sin and the need of salvation, about the Savior, the Dispensations, the story told in the Bible, the signs of the Times, the coming Tribulation Period, and the Second Coming of Christ. Be faithful in church attendance, and faithful in working for him.

"Not forsaking the assembling of ourselves together, as the manner of some is; but exhorting one another: and so much the more, as ye see the day approaching" **(Matthew 10:25).**

Jesus is coming soon. Are you ready to meet him face to face? The major portion of this work has been written as though I had presupposed every reader was already a Christian. Of course, it is not necessarily so that every Christian is fully prepared for the Lord's Return. There are certain conditions which even a redeemed person must fulfill before he can truthfully say that he is "ready" to meet the Lord without some amount of shame for the way he has conducted his life. The redemption of his soul is assured, but his reward may be very small indeed.

But, it may be that you have not yet accepted the Lord as your own personal Savior. In this case, the question of whether or not you are ready to meet God does not concern the topic of reward, but the matter of Salvation, and the eternal destiny of your soul.

God's Bible declares that the good Lord does not desire for anyone to perish. *"For God so loved the world, that he gave his only begotten Son, that whosoever believeth in him should not perish, but have everlasting life. For God sent not his Son into the world to condemn the world; but that the world through him might be saved"* **(John 3:16-17).** And, *"God commendeth his love toward us, in that, while we were yet sinners, Christ died for us"* **(Romans 5:8).** But his birth, and life, and death count for nothing in our own individual lives unless we, ourselves, truly experience a genuine spiritual rebirth.

Nicodemus, a Pharisee whom some believe to have a been very-high ranking member of the Jewish Sanhedrin, being troubled in his heart, came to Jesus by night and spoke privately with him. Jesus revealed to him that which is the most important single truth any man may know in this life, *"Except a man be born again, he cannot see the kingdom of God "***(John 3:3).** Nicodemus was very perplexed, and asked. *"How can these things be?"* Later verses in the Bible seem to imply that Nicodemus did become a Christian, but not necessarily on the same night of his visit, and only after he "spiritually" understood what Christ was talking about.

Jesus pointed to Jewish history for an example illustrating the new birth. During the forty years of wandering in the desert of Sinai, the children of Israel were at one time faced with a horrible plague of poisonous serpents. To remedy the situation, God commanded Moses to construct and to life up a brazen serpent on a pole. Anyone, bitten by a poisonous serpent, who looked in faith toward that symbol of Christ was healed.

"And as Moses lifted up the serpent in the wilderness, even so must the Son of man be lifted up: that whosoever believeth in him should not perish, but have eternal life" **(John 3:14-15).**

The spiritual rebirth is simply a matter of faith, or belief and trust in God, that he is able to perform the very thing which he has promised. The blessed power of salvation and spiritual transformation comes from God, just as the healing power for serpentine bites came from God to Israel in the wilderness. The only requirement is that we look to him for the help that we need.

"Your faith should not stand in the wisdom of men, but in the power of God" **(I Corinthians 2:5).**

"By grace are ye saved through faith; and that not of yourselves: it is the gift of God" **(Ephesians 2:8).**

Every person born into this world is born under the condemnation of original sin.

"Wherefore, as by one man sin entered into the world, and death by sin; and so death passed upon all men, for that all have sinned" **(Romans 5:12).**

It does not matter who we are, or how moral we think ourselves to be, we carry the disease of sin within our bodies, and no man of Adam's race has ever lived who has not surrendered to its influences.

"There is none righteous, no, not one" **(Romans 3:10).**

"For there is no difference: for all have sinned, and come short of the glory of God" **(Romans 3:22 & 23).**

God does not compare man with man, but man with God. For God alone is perfect and eternal. When man is compared with God, the righteousness of man is as filthy rags **(Isaiah 64:6).** It is only when we are born anew into the person of God (the Son) that we achieve the perfect righteousness necessary for eternal life, and that righteousness is not of man but of the Lord Jesus Christ.

"But of him are ye in Christ Jesus, who of God is made unto us wisdom, and righteousness, and sanctification, and redemption" **(I corinthians 1:30).**

Would you like to accept the Lord Jesus Christ as your own personal savior? You can, regardless of who you are, where you are, or what you have done with your life in the past. Christ wants to be the savior of all people who will come to him, and put their trust in him. There is no man or woman so old, or young, or hardened, or vile that Jesus does not love and desire to save. But people must turn to him of their own accord, and accept him in their own souls. Another person cannot do it for you.

By Adam's sin, death came into the world, and with it the condemnation to an eternal separation from God in hell. *"For the wages of sin is death"* (**Romans 6:23**)**,** and, *"The soul that sinneth, it shall die"* (**Ezekiel 18:20**).

Man had sinned and incurred the debt of sin, and only a man could pay this price, for the price of man's sin was the death of man. However, man could not pay the price of sin himself without suffering death, and plunging hopelessly in to the flames of Hell. A desire for this destiny to fall upon all mankind was not in the heart of God.

At a certain, precise point in history, preodained before the foundations of the world were laid, God unveiled his merciful plan and provision for the salvation of the souls of men. Jesus Christ, the Son of God, came into the world in the form of human flesh. By his virgin birth, his blood was not tainted or cursed by the blood of Adam, for the curse of sin was evidently passed from one generation to the next by the blood of the father (not through the blood of the mother, for the Bible tells us that Eve was fooled into eating of the forbidden fruit, but Adam knew what he was doing). But he was a man, as much so as any other human who had ever lived upon the earth, for he did have his mother's flesh, and that fact qualified him to pay the price of sin brought upon the world by one man's original sin. The Son of God lived a sinless life and kept himself pure, and, in April, A.D. 30, on a cross which stood on the hill of Golgotha, he paid the price by laying down his own life, making it possible for men to find redemption for their souls.

"The blood of Jesus Christ his Son cleanseth us from all sin" (**1 John 1:17**).

"In this was manifested the love of God toward us, because God sent his only begotten Son into the world, that we might live through him. Herein is love, not that we loved God, but that he loved us, and sent his Son to be the propitiation for our sins" **(I John 4:9-10).**

We now may receive his wonderful offer of redemption simply by turning to Christ and looking to him with trust as the Savior of our souls. *"For as in Adam all die, even so in Christ shall all be made alive"* **(I Corinthians 15:22).**

Who may accept Christ as Savior? The Bible makes it clear that anyone who truly wants to may come to the Lord. But in order to do this, and to experience the new birth, certain attitudes are required.

"He that cometh to God must believe that he is, and that he is a rewarder of them that diligently seek him" **(Hebrews 11:6).**

In order to accept something as fact, we must first believe that it truly exists. In order to accept Christ as the redeemer of our souls, it is evident that we must first believe in the realty of God, and that Jesus Christ is his son. The Bible does not say that we must fully understand the Trinity of God, or how the mechanics of salvation actually work. We simply acknowledge the fact that we are sinners (separated from God by sin), and that we are in need of a savior.

"Repent ye therefore and be converted" **(Acts 3:19).**

Repent, or, in other words, be truly sorry for the sin in your life. Realize and admit to yourself that your past life has been spent unprofitably, as far as eternal things are concerned, and desire and resolve to make the remaining days of your life count for something in the service of God.

The Bible tells us, *"That if thou shalt confess with thy mouth the Lord Jesus, and shalt believe in thine heart that God hath raised him from the dead, thou shalt be saved. for with the heart man believeth unto righteousness; and with the mouth confession is made unto salvation"* **(Romans 10:9-10).**

You must personally receive Christ into your heart by faith, if the new birth truly is to become a part of your life. Believe in the work that Christ has performed on the Cross. Believe that he laid down his life as a substitute for the lives of all men, and, especially, that Christ died for you! He loves you, and wants to be your Savior! He made provision for you in the blueprint of the world, he created you for a purpose, and that purpose begins with your spiritual birth into the family of God.

But you must turn to him on your own. This act of faith may be accomplished at any place or time that you are willing to turn everything over to Jesus Christ. Trust him, and come to him in faith, believing that he will do exactly as he has promised.

Several years ago, I was walking to work late one evening, and crossing over the lawn of the courthouse in Lawton, Oklahoma. It was very cold, and the ground was covered with winter ice and snow. I suddenly became aware of an unfortunate animal crying out in deep anguish and despair, and the sounds directed me toward a fishpond and fountain nearby. Looking over the wall of the pond, I discovered that a dog had somehow become entrapped in the cold and freezing water beneath me. I could not imagine how he had arrived in that situation, but I knew he was swimming for his very life, and losing, as the frigid water sapped the heat out of his body. He had momentarily rested his front paws on the edge of the center fountain piece, but it was only a short matter of time until the low temperature would cause the poor animal to slip beneath the water.

I leaned over the rocky edge of the wall as far as I could, extended my hand toward him, and called to him to come to me. He trusted me enough to forsake the small ledge that was keeping him afloat, turned toward me, and swam to a point where I was able to lift him out of the fishpond to safety.

Jesus wants us to come to him in the same manner, to turn from a world that is only temporary, and to allow him to lift us to safety. Call upon him to be your Savior. *"For whosoever shall call upon the name of the Lord shall be saved"* **(Romans 10:13).**

"All that the Father giveth me shall come to me; and him that cometh to me I will in no wise cast out" **(John 6:37).**

"Come unto me, all ye that labor and are heavy laden, and I will give you rest. Take my yoke upon you, and learn of me; for I am meek and lowly in heart: and ye shall find rest unto your souls. For my yoke is easy, and my burden is light" **(Matthew 11:28-30).**

Will you accept Christ as your own personal savior? You can, and right now. Simply speak to him, out loud or from your heart, but mean it from the depths of your soul. A hundred different people may express their individual desire in a hundred different ways, using different words, but an example of the prayer you should pray might be something like this.

"Dear Jesus, I believe that I am a lost sinner, and that you alone can save me. I believe that you paid the price of my sin when you died upon the Cross of Calvary, that you rose from the grave, and that you alone hold the power of eternal life for men. I now accept you as my own personal Savior, and trust in you from this day forward. I will also acknowledge you before others, and seek your leadership day by day. Thank you, Lord Jesus."

If you do accept the Lord Jesus as your own personal savior, it will make the author very happy to hear from you. Drop a line in the mail and let me know about your decision.

After receiving the lord Jesus as your Savior, I believe that a newborn Christian should join himself to a Bible-believing church, be baptized, and study and serve in the fellowship of other Christians. Unlike some who teach that you should join the church of your choice, I believe that you should seek out a fundamental-conservative type church which believes the Bible is the literal word of God, that salvation is by grace and not by the works of man, that the Rapture will occur before the Tribulation Period, and that Christ will return to the earth before the thousand-year Millennium unfolds. I believe that the church you attend should be strong for evangelism, seeking to spread the message of salvation both at home and to the uttermost parts of the world. I believe its membership should be friendly, slow to anger, and never self-righteous in nature. More lost people have probably been driven away from churches by better-than-thou attitudes than we would ever imagine. We should remember that the Church is based upon the love of God, and that that love should flow through every Christian out into a lost and dying world, We who call ourselves Christian are not perfect, for, we find ourselves sometimes doing the very things we know are contrary to our God's will. But, even though we may fail him, he will not forsake us. As children of mortal parents,

I am sure we often disappointed them by mistakes we made, but we were still their children and they loved us and cared for us. It is the same way with God. Even after becoming Christians, we make mistakes that hurt our fellowship with our maker, but we are still his children and he still loves us. But the Christian who intends to get serious about his life for God, and does so, will find that life will hold so much more joy and satisfaction for him.

It is high time that the churches and individual Christians of the world realize that their goals are not really as important as perhaps some once thought. Christ tells us that we should lay up for ourselves treasures in heaven. We live on the threshold of eternity, and what have we personally really done for the Lord?

"Let us lay aside every weight, and the sin which doth so easily beset us, and let us run with patience the race that is set before us **"(Hebrews 12:1).**

It is difficult to bring this particular chapter to a close, for there is so much to talk about, and so many different things to say. In the past, some, believing that the Lord would return upon a certain day or a certain time period, have laid aside the responsibilities of life and have gone out to mountain tops, or to other significant places, and have sat down, and simply waited for his appearance. I do not at all believe that this is what God would have his servants do. If a good farmer sees a severe storm threatening his ready to harvest crop, he does not sit down in a select viewing place to watch the storm come through. He makes a best effort to harvest as much of his crop as possible. I am sure that the Lord will be well pleased to find his Church striving faithfully to bring in as much of the harvest of lost souls as possible before the spiritual storm comes. Do not quit working for God, but, as long as day continues, witness to others, telling them what God has done for you.

There is a new world coming in which there will be no more heartache, sorrow, or disappointment. Christ will be the ruler of that perfect world, and the imperfections brought about by sin in this world will not exist there. In all reasonable sense, most of us have lived our lives believing that that time would come to pass someday, and we should not be surprised or shocked that it should come in our lifetime.

But it is a time for seriousness, and a time for misdirected lives to be made straight. For the Kingdom of Heaven is truly at hand.

The eternal world described in the last two chapters of the book of Revelation is beyond all the beautiful imaginations of man to fully grasp while we remain in this mortal flesh. But we accept the words of God concerning our future home with joy and happiness, because we believe him, and know that he is fully capable of creating the perfect place for us that he has promised. It is a tragedy that some people will never see that great and shinning city, or walk upon its streets of gold. But it need not be that way. God's provision has been made and offered. It is up to us to accept it, and look forward with expectation to the day when the faithful trump will sound, and the Lord will at last appear in the air!

"Behold, I stand at the door, and knock: if any man hear my voice, and open the door, I will come in to him, and will sup with him, and he with me" **(Revelation 22:20b).**

*"And at midnight there was a cry made, Behold, the bridegroom cometh; go ye out to meet him" (***Matthew 25:6).**

Surely, it is almost upon us!

*"Even so, come, Lord Jesus" (***Revelation 22:20b).**